JOURNEY OF THE HEART

Our Spiritual Memoir of Love and Loss

LYNDA SAFFELL AND MEL FERGENBAUM

JOURNEY OF THE HEART
Our Spiritual Memoir of Love and Loss
by Lynda Saffell & Mel Fergenbaum
1. FAM029000 2. OCC019000 3. BIO026000
ISBN: 978-1-949642-79-7
EBOOK: 978-1-949642-80-3

Cover design by LEWIS AGRELL

Printed in the United States of America

Authority Publishing
11230 Gold Express Dr. #310-413
Gold River, CA 95670
800-877-1097
www.AuthorityPublishing.com

To our **Higher Power**

Thank you for your loving and compassionate guidance. We are grateful for our deep connection with Source, and we trust and believe that there is a divine plan for us to be together as life partners.

Thank you to all of our friends and people we've met in our travels who, upon hearing our love story, energized us with *"What a great story. You should write a book!"* Well, here it is!

To **Cynthia Lindman, Ghostwriter**

Mel met Cynthia at a business networking meeting in Asheville, NC. Feeling an instant connection, we hired her to create an outline for our memoir. Once she heard our story, she encouraged us to publish it and offered to be our ghostwriter. Thank you for believing in us and seeing the value in sharing our journey for others to experience. You translated our memories to paper so beautifully, and we are ever grateful for your work and your friendship.

To **Stephanie Chandler** and **Chela Hardy** with Authority Publishing

Thank you for your expertise and patience in guiding us through all of the infinite details to get our book published, as well as teaching us how to promote it out into the world.

To the **RYL Communities across America**

From our roots in the Tampa Bay area and across the country, thank you for "holding the space" and creating the loving energy in the course room and in the world. By your courage to embrace and celebrate your own stories, you make it safe for others to embrace and celebrate their own stories.

And lastly, to **our family and friends**

Thank you for your love and support through the years. We are grateful to have you in our lives and to be sharing this crazy adventure called LIFE with you!

*In memory of Myrna
who lived life with a graceful strength.
She taught us to live each day to the fullest because
we don't know which will be our last.
Loving wife and friend, her unearthly visits brought us together
and inspired us to write this book.*

*In memory of Lynn Smalley
I was gifted the mother I'd always wished for at fourteen,
and she welcomed me into her heart.
She modeled for me how to be a great wife and mother
and taught us all that love, not blood, makes us family.
I love and miss you,
Lynda*

There are many great love stories,
but OURS is my favorite.

Author Unknown

CHAPTER ONE

DON'T STAY FOR ME

They came for Myrna on a Wednesday.

She was so frail they had to carry her out in a makeshift gurney fashioned by folding the corners of her favorite quilt together. The paramedics were careful to carry her slowly but Mel, Myrna's husband of forty-three years, could still hear her moan from within. He watched the quilt rock softly like a hammock as he followed them.

Myrna hadn't spoken in two days, leaving Mel to silence, to the agony of his own despairing attentiveness, and to the lone solace that her suffering would soon end. Friends brought meals daily even though she'd stopped eating solid food, and an acid fist ground the pit of his stomach whenever he dared to glance at a casserole.

The scene felt surreal. Mel's emotions rose, stuck in his throat just like they had when his mother died of cancer. Since then, he'd worked diligently to unstick them, to actually feel his feelings and express them. Now, as he followed Myrna out of the RV home they shared, he thought about how he'd say goodbye.

Until cancer, he hadn't fully realized how difficult something so simple could be. Saying goodbye.

As the small group exited the RV's narrow door, Mel stepped down into the Florida sunlight, shaded his eyes, and closed the door. It was a mild and sunny postcard March day in Tampa. Palm trees, pine, and crepe myrtle dotted the RV park. Beyond that, wild, scrubby patches of live oak and loblolly pine lined the streets, fluttering in the ocean breezes. The air was moist and sweet-smelling, its perfection in the midst of his circumstances, stinging.

This was the worst day of his life.

Along with the two EMTs, the hospice crew included a driver, who'd been waiting in the front seat with the engine idling. When he noticed them walking towards the ambulance, he hurried to meet them. He cast a hesitant smile as he opened the back doors and helped lift her in. Except for the sway of her makeshift hammock, Myrna's body, down to eighty pounds, was completely still. Mel heard a last, muffled whimper over the idling engine.

He repressed the urge to jump into the truck and hug her. He remembered one of the new rules of their world – the smallest movement, even the lightest hug, inflicted agony. The fact that he couldn't even embrace her made him feel so small and helpless as he watched the doors close on his wife.

A tiny part of him wanted to yell, admonish them to drive slowly – anything to keep her body from being jostled, to keep her from feeling any more pain. For a split second, he wondered if she was hungry or thirsty, if there was enough time to get her water cup before they drove away. But he already knew. There was no more time.

Water. That's what she'd wanted the last time they spoke a couple of days ago. The memory of that day began to replay and filled his senses as he regarded the slow, silent roll of the ambulance driving away.

He'd carried a half-filled, plastic cup with a straw into their tiny bedroom. He gently slid his hand beneath the pillow to raise her up so she could drink. As she sucked the liquid into her mouth, she no longer looked anything like herself. The disease had aged her way beyond her 64 years. Her skin had gone gray, and her head was so light, it barely made a dent in the pillow. Her eyes – once a creamy mahogany that gleamed as she danced, now hallowed by pain and medication – fixed on him as she inhaled a sharp breath of air, then let out a raspy cough. Then she spoke.

"I don't want to do this anymore," she'd said. Her voice had stretched behind them like threads unraveling in wind.

Mel heard her words but scrambled to interpret them. For eighteen months, since the day she was diagnosed, she'd said nothing about dying. Neither of them had. She'd only said, whenever the possibility of death came up, that she wasn't about to leave. She had too much to do. She'd said this so many times it began to feel like a mantra. He knew these kinds of affirmations could be easily mistaken for denial, but they were so much more than that. Each one was a deliberate choice, made over and over, to never give up. A raft in a storm, a light in the dark. As long as recovery was possible, they had both focused their whole hearts on it, admitting no other outcome, though they felt another lurking. The sicker Myrna became, it seemed an impossible contradiction for them to hold these two realities at once, their faith in recovery and their knowledge that things were going downhill.

It made him tear up a little, as he struggled to somehow forestall an ending that remained unthinkable and survive it with some kind of grace.

"I just . . . I just want to go home." Home? As all the possible interpretations raced through Mel's mind, he sensed that something which had always felt solid and true was beginning to slip away. He paused and glanced around the tiny bedroom they'd called home for the past eight months. There wasn't much to see. It was supposed to be simple, a cozy space that only had room for the things that mattered most.

He and Myrna had decided to live and travel in it almost exactly a year ago. She wanted to be with their daughter when Melanie gave birth to their grandchild. As the birth neared, Melanie and her mom talked nearly every day on the phone. Myrna was still relatively strong then, and together with Mel, she raced to empty their townhouse and get to Minnesota in time for the birth. When they finally hit the road, Melanie was already dilating so she told Myrna, *don't be disappointed if the baby arrives before you do.*

But Myrna was determined.

When the big day arrived, Myrna was right there, standing behind the doctor. Since Mel heard about all this secondhand, he couldn't remember if Myrna told him whether she greeted the baby after she heard his first cry, or if she had waited until after the doctor waved her on. He only remembered her telling him that her first words to the baby were "thanks for waiting."

So where was home? With her family in Canada, with her children, all their years together?

As he returned to her gaze, he realized the answer was right there. In her eyes. Neither of them counted themselves as religious, but they were both deeply spiritual. As he looked at her, he understood that "home" pointed to something beyond the RV, beyond this world and everything they'd built together. Something deep within him knew it was time to let go. He didn't want to – God, he didn't want to. But he had to, for both of them. It was time to say goodbye.

Mel was a man who cared deeply about truth. He'd built his entire life around knowing, speaking, and living his truth. But all those truths paled beside the truth he spoke next. It felt instinctual, as if it had lived in his heart all these years, waiting to be released.

"If you want to leave," he told her, "go. Don't stay and be in pain for me," as tears welled in his eyes. She continued resting her hand in his. They sat in silence, and then she said something else. "I want to hold the baby one last time."

He realized now, as he stared through the emptiness the ambulance left behind it, that these would probably be her last words.

She would only be in hospice one breathless day before she reached her final destination. Home.

CHAPTER TWO
MEL AND MYRNA

Mel met Myrna the year Elvis first appeared on *The Ed Sullivan Show* and beamed "Heartbreak Hotel" into the screaming hearts of girls everywhere. The Montreal Canadiens won their first of what would be seven consecutive Stanley Cups. And April broke across the St. Lawrence River and the spires of Montreal as it always did, intermingling bright, icy days with t-shirt weather, the sticky, green buds of maples unfurling above the streets.

Mel was thirteen when he lived on Rue Saint-Dominique in Mile End, a tiny enclave where it was more common to hear Yiddish than French or English. Neighborhood kids chased each other over dirty snow mounds after school. They improvised makeshift playgrounds with whatever they had at hand, and they conducted impassioned hockey matches in the streets, as mothers and aunts clipped sheets and towels to clotheslines. Families were large, cousins as plentiful as wrought-iron staircases and sidewalk weeds.

Despite all this, the kids who played on the streets of Mile End sensed the burden of their elders. They knew, some more than others, that they enjoyed the rewards of a peace hard-won by those who came before them. And if anyone could help it,

Mile End's borders were not crossed, at least not alone. When trouble threatened, as it sometimes did, the community closed around its own like an eighteenth-century wagon train, shielding its members from the long shadows of oppression too many of them, like Mel's father, had lived through.

Mel's father, Solly, had only been thirteen when he arrived in Montreal, an impoverished refugee riding the tidal wave of Jewish emigration from Eastern Europe to the New World. Solly's beginning was so different from his own that it felt distant, surreal, mythic even. Maybe this was because Solly never shared any stories about his life back in Poland and Romania, or about anything that happened afterwards. His stoicism and silence might've been more temperament than reticence, more nature than nurture. Still, Solly bore whatever wounds he had acquired mutely, and Mel was left to imagine the dark otherworld his dad came from.

Solly's given name was Srul. His mother and siblings arrived after him, piecemeal, whenever the Jewish aid society could sponsor them. It was from this precarious background that Srul grew into a kind, taciturn, hard-working man. Perhaps when he listened quietly to his thirteen-year-old son's stories of a "first girlfriend," he secretly thrilled at the wonderful, silly privilege of a teenage crush. But if he did, he remained outwardly unmoved, except to gruffly inquire why Mel needed a girlfriend so early, anyhow. Like many in the community, Solly was staunchly traditional. It was how they all survived. Boyfriends existed to become husbands, fathers, providers, and workers. Girlfriends existed to become wives, mothers, and homemakers. Seen in this light, thirteen was indeed awfully young to court a marriage prospect.

Of course, Mel, being only thirteen, didn't know or care if it was too soon or not. He just knew Myrna was pretty. She was sweet. And he liked the idea of her, just as he liked the idea of his own parents who taught him every day through their restrained, wordless devotion that relationships lasted forever.

Even though Mel often felt shy like his dad, he felt comfortable in his group, and it seemed he was always surrounded by friends, always moving within a flock of kids that roamed the winding lanes of Mile End together. It was in one of these groups that Mel first noticed Myrna. She was walking with his best friend.

He noticed her ponytail of shiny, rich brown hair and her blue jeans. She had an unusually stylish flair for a fourteen-year-old girl from Mile End. He asked his friend to introduce them, and later that evening, when the gang attended a youth dance, Mel discovered that she just happened to be the best jitterbug dancer on the floor.

He, on the other hand, had two left feet.

Content to watch her from the shadows of the sidelines and mingle with his friends, he jumped at an opportunity to walk her home. He told her she was a swell dancer. Then she suggested they dance sometime. He could almost feel his ears turn red. As much as he'd like to learn, he remarked sheepishly, he really didn't know a thing about it. They were standing in front of her staircase and when she heard this, she grabbed his hand and offered to teach him right there.

She was a patient teacher, going slow, and repeating steps so he could keep up. She never lost her breath, but her eyes, lit beneath the streetlamp, took his away.

Myrna made it official the next day at school when she proclaimed to everyone that Mel was her boyfriend. They hadn't talked about their attraction at all. They had especially avoided all talk of couples, boyfriends, and girlfriends. But it happened anyway. They began a relationship with an improvised jitterbug lesson on a cold Spring night, their breaths merging in a moist pocket of air between them.

Myrna's Sweet 16 with Mel

CHAPTER THREE
GONE HOME

Myrna was alone in the room when Mel came in. Her eyes were closed, and she appeared to be resting comfortably. But sleeping wasn't exactly the best word for what was happening.

The hospice room was stock medical issue, a monochrome wash of green and gray. Mel winced at the IV tubes pumping liquids and medications into her veins, the sound of her ventilator harsh and loud. Even though it all made him uncomfortable, he felt a surge of relief as he dropped his things in a chair and sat on the bed beside her.

She was still alive. And she wasn't in pain.

Two days earlier he'd placed two long-distance phone calls, one to his son Mark in Denver and one to Melanie in Minnesota. Both would need as much time as possible to fly to Tampa. Like everyone else, they'd feared this was coming for a while, but neither were truly ready. How could they be? Then a call to Mitch who wouldn't have to travel, as he was the only one who still lived close by.

The next phone call was to his teaching partner Cindy. It was a blanket alert and invitation to everyone in their close-knit community that they had built over the past nine years. He told her to tell anyone else who wanted to visit Myrna where she was. Now, as he gazed at her helplessly, the relatively practical concerns about who would arrive in time to say goodbye began to fade, and he dissolved into the present moment.

The entire time Mel sat beside her, she didn't stir. Not even an eyelash. There seemed to be no sign that she even knew he was with her. Wondering if touch might rouse her, he cupped one of her hands in his. It drooped warm and soft. He kissed her wrist, feeling the faint flush of blood moving under her skin. If she couldn't wake up, he hoped she could at least hear or sense his presence. He'd read somewhere that hearing was the last thing to go, so he reasoned she might still be able to hear him. After all, there was no evidence to the contrary, and it was better than imagining the alternative, that he'd never be able to connect with her again.

He sat like this for a long time, and as he did, a mental collage began knitting together in his mind. Made of imprints, words, feelings, and memories long forgotten and long cherished, the pieces joined together and projected on an inner screen. An ephemeral snippet of conversation, the flashing of a smile. The cry of a newborn baby, the sound of the sea.

Moments of anger, stupid mistakes, derision, laughter, an embrace.

He barely had time to grasp any of the particulars before each memory faded into the next and dissipated, like the notes of a song passing too quickly to hold.

In the midst of his reverie, he rested his chin in his palm and listened to the syncopated heave of the ventilator. He still felt a little like he had when they put her into the ambulance... restless, incomplete, as if there was still something that needed to be said. Or maybe, she had something she still needed to hear. Myrna had always grounded him. Always. Even now he felt the pull of their shared history expand beneath him like roots, all their small habits of daily living stringing the years together like life itself. He leaned down to whisper in her ear.

The moment for goodbye had come.

"Before you go, I need to tell you – it's been an awesome ride. I would do it again in a heartbeat and –." He began to cry, then paused to collect himself. Her eyes remained closed, her touch unresponsive. He squeezed her hand as if to send a message across whatever divide had spread between them.

"I would do it all over again, Myrna, and I would do it with you." His face crumpled, tears spilling down his face. They were the cleansing, grief-engorged tears of a broken heart, but not of a broken man.

Over the next few hours, a few close friends arrived, and despite his shock, or maybe because of it, it felt easy to console them. Perhaps this was more of a surprise for them than for him. After all, he'd been her caretaker for a year and a half, enduring, hoping, and fighting beside her. He'd had all that time to reckon with this moment, if only semi-consciously. But when Mitch and his family arrived, it was Mel's two young grandchildren that undid him. He hugged them, telling them, "If you want to say anything to Bubbie, now would be a good time." Melanie arrived next, her eyes red-rimmed and tender. Mel advised her that the nurses told him Myrna could go any minute. Melanie held her baby, Joshie, on her hip then placed him in Mel's lap. As Mel looked into the baby's eyes, it dawned on him. Joshie, now eight months, was the grandchild Myrna had rushed to meet, had thanked for waiting for her. Now, Myrna seemed to be waiting for Joshie.   Holding Joshie had been her last wish. Remembering this, he knew what to do.

Everyone grew quiet and watched Mel clasp Joshie's tiny hand to Myrna's. Joshie's palm felt like a damp starfish, Myrna's like crumpled paper. Their hands stayed like this for a moment or two, until Joshie began to whimper, and Mel lifted him into his Dad's arms.

And just as he did, Myrna took one breath. Then one more. And then her breath fell silent.

The room erupted into muffled embraces. Only when everyone was gone, and after each had said goodbye in their own way, did Mel take Myrna's hand one last time. It was the same warm hand that led him through his first dance lesson under a street lamp so many years ago in a spring that would always be theirs. A part of him couldn't believe it was over.

As he rose and took his first steps away from her, he turned to see a thick tear squeezing itself from her eye, trickling towards the bed.

Myrna had gone home.

CHAPTER FOUR
STRING TO MY BALLOON

Everyone in the family had a first name that started with M.

Mark was born first, followed by Mitch, and finally Melanie. Mark was creative, sensitive, and cerebral. He acquired the nickname "Stormy" because so many of his birth ceremonies happened under stormy skies. Mel later revised it to "Sunshine." Mitch, "Happiness", was the wild one, rambunctious and social. And Melanie was the baby. Flamboyant, outspoken, and keen on fashion, she garnered the nickname "Princess" and gravitated towards her older brother Mark from an early age.

Like their parents before them, Mel and Myrna were traditional. He worked while she stayed home to raise the children. She grew into one of those warm mothers who created the home all the neighborhood kids wanted to visit. Her own family had been similar: generous, expressive, and loving. But, they didn't seem to expect anything more for Myrna than motherhood. They supported her decision to drop out of school in tenth grade. Her path was already laid out. All she had to do was follow it.

Mel's family was just as conventional, but where Myrna's was warm, his ran cool. There wasn't a lot of talk in his house, especially about feelings. Solly, perhaps believing that men didn't verbalize feelings, never even told Mel or his younger brother that he loved them. And in both Mel and Myrna's families, the men made the final decisions, played head of household.

Every day, Mel went to work, believing that it was his sole responsibility to provide for his family. Each night when he got home, he'd sit down and watch the sunset or read the sports pages while Myrna made dinner. Just like his dad, he didn't really talk about feelings and, for a long time, he didn't get it when she did. "What do you have to cry about?" he'd implore. "You have a husband, three beautiful children, and a nice home." He didn't have the ability to see things from her perspective, to understand how she was feeling.

Still, despite their traditional roles, both Mel and Myrna also wanted to be more open-minded and modern than their parents. They wanted each member of the family to feel and be equally valuable, capable of determining and steering their own courses. Mel wanted his children, especially the boys, to feel comfortable expressing themselves despite the fact that he, like Solly, didn't really do that himself. He also wanted his kids to know they were loved. So, unlike Solly, he told them often that he loved them. For her part, Myrna encouraged all the kids, especially Melanie, to have dreams and to believe they were capable of achieving them.

One time, in the spirit of innovation, they conducted an experiment. Wanting to teach the children about fairness, Mel and Myrna held a family meeting and introduced a new concept, the family democracy. They'd make decisions together and each member would get a single vote, with the majority winning. The first decision was practical, the vote smooth. Together, the family voted on whether or not someone had to ask to share someone else's toys. Mel couldn't help being reminded of a time when he was the oldest brother going out of his way to share his toys with his little brother. He'd always wanted, more than anything else, for his parents to be proud of him, to be a "good boy."

The next day, emboldened by their initial success, Mel's brood met him at the door after work with a new proposal. Mark, the spokesperson for his younger siblings, said, "We need to talk to you about something, Dad." Mel put his briefcase down, took off his shoes, and commenced the democratic meeting. Mark began, "Us three had a meeting today while you were at work, and we all decided that we wanted to call a vote on an allowance raise." Mel raised his eyebrows. He was truly surprised.

"An allowance raise?"

"Yes, and since we have majority, it's three against two." Mel could see Melanie peeking out from behind her big brother. Mitch sat on the floor fidgeting. Mel didn't want to dash his kids' hopes. He even felt proud of them for being savvy enough to use the rules of the system to get what they wanted. He and Myrna hadn't actually thought through the fact that the kids outnumbered them, and they might be clever enough to figure it out.

And that was the end of that experiment.

As the years passed, Mel became more spontaneous and free-spirited, but he could also be impulsive and thoughtless. Myrna tended to be more conservative, often playing the voice of reason. He came to think of her as the string to his balloon. He valued the way she grounded him but often longed for freedom. Not from her – just freedom. He was never sure if this came from the prescribed social roles they fell into, their personalities, or the simple inevitability of life stages. Whatever the case, nothing, not his family or society, prepared him to deal with the emotional tides of marriage or swim the deeper waters of intimacy.

Because he didn't know how to deal with emotions, he retreated in the face of Myrna's, or was outright insensitive to them. Over time, she grew resentful and shut down in return. More and more, Mel became withdrawn, emotionally unavailable, and rigid. Even his kids sometimes saw him this way. Feeling dissatisfied with the lack of passion and intimacy in their marriage, but not understanding why or what to do about it, he eventually became sexually involved with a co-worker.

Meanwhile, Myrna, craving emotional intimacy and processing her own anger, started her own affair.

In the end, their overly scripted roles and their individual choices had created happiness, then hollowness, then distance.

Perhaps Myrna, who'd always been reliable and self-sacrificing, needed to feel her boldness, her selfishness even. Making a choice on her own behalf, to allow herself something she alone wanted, was revolutionary for her. Her choice confronted Mel, the thinker and doer, with the emotional fallout of his own indiscretions and unavailability. Together, they faced a choice.

They could either address the causes of the rupture or go their separate ways. They chose forgiveness and embraced change. Over time, he learned how to be more emotionally available, and she learned to ask for the things she wanted and needed. Still, he was hardly emotionally sensitive or expressive. And she was a long way from empowered.

True change for them both would come years later after they reconciled, moved from the snows of Montreal to Florida, and finished raising their children. And it would all start with a class called *Understanding Yourself and Others*.

CHAPTER FIVE

ICE MAN

UYO, as it was commonly called, was an unabashed, unapologetic self-development program. The problem was that Mel didn't "need" self-development. He had participated in *Marriage Encounter* in the '70s and EST in the '80s, but things were good now. He wouldn't ever have taken the course if Mark and Melanie hadn't experienced it first and persuaded him and Myrna to enroll. He didn't have a problem with self-development. He just thought it was unnecessary at this point in his life.

Of course, he knew Myrna and his kids had opinions about his shortcomings, but he was only human. And as far as he was concerned, he'd already done the growth needed. It had been years since his and Myrna's crisis, and they had long since forgiven one another and moved on. They now owned their own business, a Stewart Oxygen Services franchise. They made a great team as Myrna handled the administrative duties from their office, and Mel made sales calls and taught classes in their territory. If Myrna was happy, or if he was happy, he wasn't always sure. But he knew they weren't unhappy.

He'd always had a way of figuring things out, of getting what he wanted out of life. Wasn't that happiness? Still, he had to admit that sometimes, he had the feeling he was floundering in some way – that he was not getting what he really wanted. Then again, he figured that was life. Ultimately, he believed he had what he needed to make a happy life.

It felt a little more like UFO than UYO on the first day of class. Mel sized up his classmates and observed to learn the customs. He conversed mildly with fellow students and even felt sincerely curious about why they were there. But when the instructor invited them to "process," his moment was upon him. He knew "processing" meant that he had to talk about his feelings. He reassured himself that it would be over quickly because he didn't have any particular issues to process. To be considerate to the other students and get himself out of the way, he decided to go first.

The instructor asked him why he came and how he was feeling about life. He was fine, Mel told him, and had no particular feelings to discuss. Waiting for this fact to become clear to the instructor, Mel responded blandly to more questions. An hour dragged by. Then another. Mel began to feel deflated. The entire time, he could not for the life of him figure out what he was supposed to be processing or why.

Finally, his instructor looked at him and said, "I know what your issue is, buddy. You don't have blood in your veins. You have ice in your veins."

Mel was stunned. He wanted to defend himself. Of course he had feelings. He was only human, after all. But when he tried to recall recent times when he felt emotional, he stumbled. Slowly, in the midst of all his classmates and fellow seekers, it dawned on him that maybe the instructor was right. He was flatline.

How had it happened?

Myrna, who gazed at him from her chair, was his comfort. Her eyes glistened with love but also with knowing. She seemed to be waiting for something, waiting for him to get it. Hadn't she said various versions of this to him over the years? Hadn't it almost broken their family apart once?

Speechless, he ended the "processing" and silently promised himself he would do whatever it took to address his problem.

He thought of his dad Solly, who never told his kids he loved them, never even hugged them. Shy to the point of pain, Solly submerged his emotions for reasons that still remained mysterious to Mel. Maybe it was early trauma back in Poland and Romania, or having to survive in a new country alone. Maybe it had something to do with being a man, with being strong. Maybe it was just his innate personality.

Mel choked up as he thought about the fact that he'd never actually know the answer. Even if he asked, Solly would never open up and tell him.

Solly was the original Iceman.

And all these years Mel had been walking blindly in his footsteps. But he wanted something different for his life. He wanted to change.

The next day, the instructor led the class through several "life purpose" exercises, something Mel might've scoffed at only two days before. Mel already knew he didn't want to be an "iceman", and he knew he couldn't spend his life blaming the fact that he was on his dad or anyone else. But when he thought about what he wanted his life purpose to be, he wasn't sure. He just knew it would be the opposite of what he'd already created – a life devoid of passion, one shaped by unquestioned beliefs, by roads well worn. He also knew he wanted to experience life fully, and that meant feeling it completely, not shoving it away because he was uncomfortable or afraid.

Then he realized that was his answer. It was so simple.

He picked up his notebook and wrote, "I want Passion in my life." Passion, with a capital P.

Within a few years, Passion led him, over-thinking, rational Mel, to a new career and a new life. He learned how to recognize, experience, and talk about his feelings. He began to develop a deeper connection to himself and to life that made him feel passionate with a P, including Myrna. Then, inspired to help others create the kinds of change they desired in their lives, he trained to be a UYO instructor. He was officially a proud, card-carrying convert to self-development. It was when he started teaching UYO that he met his future business partner, Cindy.

From the very beginning, Cindy impressed him. He knew her by reputation long before they met. She was widely known and respected as a UYO instructor. She'd been instructing longer than he had, and she'd even helped mentor him. At first, he and Cindy were just friends, but the more he thought about it, the more he thought she'd make a great business partner. Like Mel, she trusted her instincts, but she was also direct and would hold people accountable, two things that weren't always Mel's strong suit. Married with two grown daughters, Cindy was also fastidious. She always looked the part. It didn't take long for them to start talking about a common dream, to one day be full-time instructors helping others create real happiness. When Mel worked up the financials, they quickly saw the potential.

They incorporated, and together, they created a new self-development course that evolved over time, and they renamed it *Redirect Your Life*.

As for Myrna, she was slightly less impressed with Cindy, aware that she never fully carried her share of the business responsibility. It was Mel and Myrna who handled all the "behind-the-scenes" details. Still, Myrna steadfastly supported their new direction and business, and defined her own role within it. She kept an open heart and mind, and focused on the next chapter.

CHAPTER SIX

PASSION AND PURPOSE

Change your mind, change your life.

This was the motto of *Redirect Your Life*.

The course took place over a weekend during which Mel and Cindy coached students on exactly how they could practice this deceptively simple teaching. The students hailed from all walks of life and carried nearly every situation and mindset possible into the course room in the hopes of transformation. Unresolved questions, painful stories, deep patterns of belief, things forgotten, left undone, left unsaid, grief and loss. It was all fodder.

Many did transform, but it was usually less epiphany and more process, a long process where they practiced a new way of *being*, both in and out of the course room. This is why many graduates returned month after month to volunteer or even "review" the course. Before long, the two kids from Mile End had surrounded themselves with another crowd, a community based on love, warmth, fellowship, and most importantly, acceptance. Mel did his best to learn, practice, and embody the RYL teachings. It was the journey taken with sincerity, and not the ideal, that mattered most. Most of all, at least for him, it was about authenticity and integrity.

As instructors, Mel and Cindy entered each weekend with a loose format, guiding principles, and a toolkit of potential exercises. But it was the students in each course who set the tone. Maybe this was why it became so successful. Over time, many of the graduates came to view Mel and Cindy as a sort of "mom and dad" of the community. And they affectionately called him and Myrna "M & M." Mel and Cindy taught the course every month without fail, and Myrna never missed one, no matter what.

Over time, and with the support of her RYL practices, she grew to appreciate and accept Cindy, but she never completely left behind her initial impression. All the things that had attracted Mel to Cindy as a business partner and instructor were still true, but she also seemed to hold herself above others at times.

It was in the little things, like sitting in higher chairs than the students or conferring favor on certain assistants. Originally, Mel and Cindy planned to share profits and responsibilities equally, but as time went on, Mel ended up handling most of the work that built the business and kept it running. He hustled to recruit most of the students each month and stayed on top of planning and logistics. Even with volunteers it was a lot of work. Eventually, they agreed his profit share should be slightly higher than fifty percent, but sometimes, he felt it still didn't truly reflect the amount of work he put in.

Nevertheless, it seemed like a very small price to pay for living his vision. And he and Cindy were great friends, so it was easy enough to overlook the imbalance. Along with Myrna and the students, they were building a values-based community, an experiment that had become successful. He kept his focus on serving the students, and when he wasn't instructing, on his own growth and Passion.

If Mel's purpose was Passion, Myrna's might've been *Personal Power*. Through RYL, all the years of feeling helpless or dis-empowered in the face of tradition melted away. She learned how to embrace her own path and became the stronger version of herself she'd always wanted to be. She was still loving, quiet, strong, and grounded. But through RYL she evolved into a woman people looked up to and appreciated. Mel joyfully referred to her as the "E.F. Hutton of the course room." When she talked, people listened. Some assistants even gave her a nickname: The Rock.

Myrna and Mel also evolved spiritually. Before UYO, he never thought much about God. God had always been about rules and custom, not personal connection. But living with Passion cultivated his spiritual side. It required faith and the ability to surrender control, something he knew he needed to practice. He read many spiritual books and began referring to a Higher Power as "Upper Management." He also formed a philosophy about life that mirrored his teaching work. He came to believe that "learning and teaching" was the ultimate purpose of life, and Upper Management was the ultimate teacher. Myrna believed similarly, though she also continued to practice many of the religious traditions with which she grew up.

For years, neither of them had been quite so happy, until one windy September day when it all turned upside down.

CHAPTER SEVEN
ALL THE PRAYERS

The first time either Mel or Myrna heard the word *adenocarcinoma*, it was storm season, 2004. It was a word doctors used when the fluid-producing glands that line an organ develop cancerous cells. It can develop into lesions or tissue growth, but it doesn't start there. It starts with an overproduction of fluid and then it slowly drowns the body from the inside.

Myrna and Mel had just returned to their townhouse from visiting family in Toronto. They'd strategically timed their trip to escape the hurricanes and tropical storms churning off the Florida coast. Myrna was carrying her purse up a flight of stairs that led from the garage to the living room. Mel, following closely behind, lugged their bags. Then Myrna suddenly stopped in the middle of the staircase.

Her purse fell down a stair, then another. A tangle of keys tumbled at her feet. Their M & M candy dispenser glinted from the landing as Myrna crumpled against the wall to her right, hunching over her stomach. When Mel asked her what was wrong, she turned around with a pinched and confused expression.

"I think I need to go to the doctor," she said.

Days later, she sat beside Mel in a dark room scrutinizing an X-ray of her lungs. A doctor pointed at shadowy smudges with his pen.

"It's a very common form of lung cancer," he told them. "But it normally occurs in smokers."

"Well then how did I get it?" Myrna asked, her voice distressed. She'd never smoked.

"It's a mystery. All we know is that a small percentage of nonsmokers develop it somehow. The first thing we need to do is get some further testing and start treatment."

"Wait," Mel interrupted, "is this . . . what's the prognosis?"

"That's hard to say because we don't know what stage it's in yet. But this form of cancer usually flies under the radar for a long time before it shows symptoms. The average five-year survival rate is low . . . but again, we don't know if that applies to your wife at this time." As she listened, Myrna kept her gaze fixed on the doctor. When she spoke, her tone was even and controlled.

"Well, what is the survival rate for most people?" The doctor paused and cleared his throat.

"About eighteen percent," he answered. Myrna shook her head.

"I'm sorry, doctor, but I'm not going anywhere. I have too much to live for."

There are as many ways to face news of cancer as there are people. Myrna met hers with determination. From the beginning, she wanted to tell everyone. *I want all the prayers*, she would say. But the way she chose to tell people was very unique. She and Mel decided to be very intentional with their language, to use language as a tool to help fight the cancer itself.

For example, when Myrna shared her news, she was careful to avoid saying, "I have cancer." Instead, she would say, "I've been diagnosed with cancer." And if she forgot, Mel gently reminded her.

It might've seemed strange to some, but they saw it as a way to acknowledge the diagnosis without *owning* the illness. They wanted to use language that reflected their hope, not their fear. And they knew they were in for the fight of their lives.

They wanted to be in that eighteen percent.

Mel pulled Mitch in to help with their oxygen franchise, so he could focus on Myrna. He still planned to instruct RYL each month, while Mitch took over the day-to-day operations of the business.

Within weeks of her diagnosis, doctors tried to remove the cancerous fluid by scraping it from the lining of her lungs. In theory, this surgery, when combined with chemotherapy, could prevent the cancer from metastasizing. It could also offset the problems that extra fluid caused in her body. But this wasn't what happened.

The surgery left her nerve endings and tissues so badly damaged that her lungs never healed. She developed a raspy, persistent cough, and the cancer gained ground as storm season came and went.

Through the winter and spring, she grew slightly weaker and often experienced pain, but overall, she still remained relatively vibrant. She continued attending each RYL course just like she always had. But summer brought a new problem. Melanie was having her first baby, and Myrna's doctor wouldn't allow her to fly to attend the birth. So, at what felt like the last minute, she and Mel rented out their townhouse, moved into a used RV, and drove to Minnesota to attend the baby's birth.

Living and traveling in an RV was one of her dreams, so what better time than now?

They stayed a month with Melanie, even upgrading to a spacious, new RV that quickly acquired the nickname "The Loft." Myrna stayed on her medications, but the business of driving jarred her body fiercely, and it didn't take much. A too sharp turn or bump and she'd be wincing or holding her side. But she never complained. And she never mentioned dying.

Of course, Mel knew that she probably experienced moments of anger or bitterness. It was only normal. Yet, he only witnessed it one time, when they were in a restaurant, seated at a table by the window. Myrna picked at her food, quieter than normal, and kept glancing out the window.

There was a woman outside smoking.

Without turning her head to look at him she blurted angrily, "I don't smoke. I have lung cancer. She smokes, and she's okay."

In that moment, Myrna's illness felt so unfair to them both. Life continued on around them as if nothing had changed. However, they'd both lived long enough to know life isn't always fair, and sometimes there are no explanations. It was the great, bittersweet trade-off we all make eventually.

Mel's anger was mostly directed at the doctors, who never seemed able to help Myrna, and didn't offer to explore alternative therapies or solutions. Ultimately, if Myrna's time on earth was complete, it wasn't for Mel to decide or rail against. All he could do was help her as much as possible and try to make sure she never felt alone. It had taken him so many years to fully show her his love. As helpless as he often felt, he was determined to show it to the very end, whenever that end happened to be.

Her decline continued, and they returned to Florida in winter after seven months on the road. They continued living in the Loft, and in February, Myrna missed an RYL course for the first time.

By March, she was gone.

CHAPTER EIGHT
LOST GOODBYES

"Family only?" Lynda asked quietly into the phone. She felt blood rushing to her head.

"Yes, it would just be easier on the family to be left alone," Carol answered. Carol, another grad of the RYL Course, was renting Mel and Myrna's Indian Shores townhouse. Lynda was scheduled to prepare and deliver a meal to Mel and Myrna's the following night, but now Carol was telling her that Myrna was being moved to hospice, and Mel shouldn't take calls. She wanted to cry as she hung up the phone.

Now, she would have no way to say goodbye or tell Mel how sorry she was.

She just couldn't believe this was happening. It almost didn't make sense. All the years Lynda had known Myrna, she'd always been so vibrant and healthy.

Then one day Myrna called to tell her she was sick. Lynda was standing in the kitchen looking out the front window when she heard Myrna say, *I have lung cancer.* Then Lynda overheard Mel in the background correcting her. Then, *I'm sorry – I've been diagnosed with lung cancer.* Even in that terrible moment, Lynda had been so sure that her friend would beat it. Now, she shook her head in shock and put her forehead in her hands. Feeling inexplicably remorseful, she recalled the last time she saw Myrna at one of the RYL courses.

Myrna sat on Lynda's right. She was dressed nicely as always, but Lynda could tell she hadn't paid as much attention to her hair as she usually did, and she wasn't wearing any makeup. Her skin was ashen and sleep clustered in the corners of her eyes. Every so often she'd doze off, unable to escape the heavy sedation of her pain medications. They didn't talk much. Lynda remembered putting her arm around Myrna's shoulders to comfort her. Then at lunch break, Carol grew upset because Myrna kept falling asleep, and Carol felt that Myrna didn't really want to be there. She told Mel that she was taking Myrna home. Lynda remembered his reply. *But she asked to be here.*

Lynda sighed and dialed her fiancé's number to tell him Myrna was going to hospice. Wade had always been the funny one, the life of the party. Now, she heard sadness in his voice. But she also knew that he'd never become as close to Myrna and Mel as she had. Over the years, she'd gone on camping trips with them, double dates, hung out at parties, and of course, been in the course room many times. Whenever she'd go to their house, she'd stop by the candy dispenser Mel and Myrna kept filled with M & M's, and every time, it would release precisely six candies. M & M. Mel and Myrna.

Lynda had always dreamed of a relationship like theirs. She knew they'd had their problems, but she could barely imagine it. Those had happened long before she knew either of them. Mel was like a really wise, big brother to Lynda, and Myrna was always so sweet and grounded, like the sister she never had. Myrna was the kind of person who did more than wait for her turn to speak. She really listened.

"It just seems like she's been connected to every important moment of my life over the past few years," she heard herself tell Wade as her voice cracked. Mel and Myrna had counseled her and Wade through a few rough spots in their relationship before they'd married. And when they did get legally married it was a secret, an elopement of sorts. The only people who knew their secret were Mel, who officiated, Myrna, who witnessed, and the reverend present.

The marriage, which had taken place only three months before, was a practical affair that helped them finance things like home renovations and a big, snazzy wedding ceremony scheduled to take place later. They continued to live in separate homes, and even though she and Wade were now legally married, they still considered themselves "engaged." Lynda started to cry into the phone.

"I'm not sure I can handle this. Losing Myrna... and all the wedding planning I have to do. I'm still trying to figure out how to pay for it. And then there's Billy . . ." she said before trailing off. Billy was her fifteen-year old son who'd just dropped out of high school. She and Wade had been arguing about how to help him. Wade wanted to send him to military school while Lynda thought RYL might help him more.

"Look, don't bring Billy into this, especially if it's only going to upset you. And you know Myrna has been dying for a long time now. It's sad but it's part of life. We have our own wedding to look forward to, don't we?" Lynda wasn't sure how to respond. She loved Wade, but his lack of empathy offered her no comfort. She felt a distance between them when she wanted closeness and support. After they ended the call, she found herself speaking to no one in particular.

"I'm not even going to get to say goodbye," she whispered into the empty room.

Myrna and Lynda at an RYL gathering. This photo sits on Mel's desk in a frame that says "Friends are Angels following you through life."

CHAPTER NINE
WISH YOU WERE HERE

Lynda grew up in a time when men walked on the moon, color TV mesmerized suburban families across America, and *The Beatles* lit beacons of rebellion and liberation never seen before. Doctors prescribed valium to repressed housewives like sweet tarts, and the city of Tampa, with its shiny Thunderbird dealership, new amusement park, and sunny beaches, looked like an idyllic Florida postcard that read, "Wish you were here." Still, all this paled beside Lynda's adoration of her father. Maybe other men walked on the moon, but Lynda's dad hung the moon itself.

He called her "my little monkey," and taught her to ride a bike. As a business owner, Bill worked long hours during the week, but on the weekends he was the fun dad who took his kids, and any of their friends who happened to be hanging around, on outings to play Gooney Golf or to ride go-carts. She was so proud he was her dad, and a bit in awe of him.

Conversely, life with her mother had been a rocky road. Although the life of the party with her friends, Mary Ann could be moody and sometimes mean, and each morning Lynda was on alert and treading lightly to sense which "mom" she was that day.

She desperately wanted her mother's love, and for years she blamed herself when she didn't get it. If she could only be a better daughter, she deduced, then her mom would be a better mom. She tried so hard to please her mom, to be the perfect daughter, but it was never enough. "You're too chubby" or "You should know better." Through her sadness, Lynda could only hear criticism. On top of that, her mother was so uncomfortable with her own feelings, she unknowingly stifled those of her children. "Young lady, you have no right to be angry," was a mantra.

Suffering from an undiagnosed form of mental illness, Mary Ann treated her anxiety with alcohol. The stress of raising three small children took a toll on her, and her evening cocktails became an oasis for her. She could escape into sweet numbness, washing away her frustrations and feelings of emptiness inside. And over time one drink became two...two became three... happy hour started earlier and earlier. Though once close and very much in love, Mary Ann and Bill began arguing more, sometimes fighting loudly in the middle of the night.

Then one day, after yet another heated argument with her mother, Lynda's father packed a suitcase, walked down the stairs to where she stood, and hugged her. She began to cry.

"Daddy, don't go!" she pleaded. "Please!" She was only twelve. How would she live without him, and what would happen if he left her and her little brothers alone with their mother? He ran a trembling hand through her ginger hair, walked back upstairs, and unpacked. But within a year he'd carry his suitcase back down the stairs and this time, he'd keep going.

Lynda's assessment, the one that played in her mind like a scratched record, was that he didn't love *her* enough to stay. This thought, though it was untrue, sunk into her heart, validating her beliefs and low sense of self-worth. Even though she visited him every weekend after that, life in her nice south Tampa home would never be the same.

For Mary Ann and her friends, life was always exciting, boozy, and brazen. There were always parties to go to, men to see, cocktails to mix. Lynda often got the feeling her mom was grooming her to be just like her. Lynda's clothes were too prudish, and her mom encouraged her to dress sexier. She coached Lynda to put on a pretty face because, as she explained it, Lynda had "the kind of face that just needed makeup." Her mom loved her in the best way she was capable of, but Lynda was too young to understand. And the angry part of her that would always feel deprived of the mother she needed, and of a normal childhood, didn't care.

When Lynda fell in love and married, her first husband wasn't like her mother. He hid the drinking from her.

For the first seven years, they had an ideal relationship. An Air Force man, he was kind, gentle, and loved their two children. Even when he was gone for long periods, she had the support of other families wherever they were stationed. The red flags started waving when she noticed the distinct smell of alcohol in his morning coffee. He began getting in trouble at work, and was eventually ordered to rehab.

Always, Lynda believed that they could make it through anything, and that if she supported him enough, he'd be able to recover. Her belief that he used alcohol to self-medicate anxiety only reinforced her commitment. Besides, when she got married she told herself it would be forever. She never wanted to get divorced like her parents did, even though now she understood her mom was the reason her dad left.

Confident in their love, Lynda wasn't too worried at all when the "for worse" part began.

For too many years, she did everything she could to support his recovery, but he continued to succumb to his disease. Running on the toxic fumes of false hope, she still believed that if she could be a better wife and support him, he would heal, and their marriage would be happy again. But those fumes became thinner and thinner, finally dissipating for good. She and the kids lost the battle to his self-destructive behavior, his disease. Her decision to finally leave was an agonizing one that crash-landed her dream of having a happy family unblemished by divorce.

One night after they separated, she sobbed on the ceramic tiles of her kitchen floor, trying to muster every ounce of strength she had so she would not pick up the phone, dial his number, and reconcile. So she would not try to rescue him again. By then, the choice was painfully clear: rescue him, or rescue herself and her kids. Her mother had wired every cell of her body to choose others over herself, to try to rescue the unrescuable, even if it might mean harming herself. But despite waffling in a twelve-year marriage long past its expiration date, that night on the kitchen floor she chose herself.

It was the hardest thing she had ever done.

CHAPTER TEN

ALLIGATOR VILLAGE

"But you don't understand!" Lynda heard herself exclaim to her life coach. "If I had a better mother, I would be a better person!"

They sat across from one another in a bookstore in Tampa a few years after her first marriage ended. That marriage had shown her that she needed to work on and support herself, not others. She needed to learn how to create the life of her dreams with an equal partner, someone who'd give her as much as he took. But when she heard herself blame her problems on her mom, she knew, in her heart of hearts, that she really *believed* this – *and* that it was an unhealthy belief.

Ultimately, even after all the work she'd done, she still hadn't forgiven her mom. And she hadn't forgiven herself for being her mother's daughter.

By the time she walked into her inaugural RYL course in 2000, it was a new century. She wanted to learn how to love and accept herself, and she was committed to doing whatever it took. Right away, RYL felt like a beautiful cocoon of love and acceptance. She began assisting whenever she could, and she bonded with many of the women in the community. Of course, everyone in the community was a flawed human being, but they were also devoted to practicing the basic principles of RYL: that you could have the life you wanted if you were willing to "do the work" to change yourself. RYL felt a lot like church, only better, and without the church.

She also loved the social aspects of it. There were regular gatherings and events like Myrna and Mel's annual Fourth of July parties at the beach. Or exclusive women's weekends for certain members of the community. She especially loved getting together to watch football, so when the Tampa Bay Buccaneers were in the Super Bowl playoffs, Lynda spared no time in scheduling an all-day party at her house. The entire city was rallying for its home team, and as a sports fan and one-time professional football cheerleader, she wasn't about to be left out.

Wade was officially the funniest guy she knew. Dressed in team colors of black, red, and pewter, he filled the room with laughter and jokes. A casual friend from childhood, she'd known him most of her life. He'd also started working with her a few years back at the local YMCA, and his warm, endearing per-sonality slowly transformed familiarity into a mild crush. At her Superbowl party, it was hard not to fall for him.

Later, after everyone else left, they stole a kiss in the kitchen and expressed their growing attraction. He seemed so genuine when he made her promises. *I'll never cheat on you. I'll never mistreat you.* In that moment, it seemed like he could be the perfect match, the partner she'd dreamt of. She had prayed for God to send her a relationship that would create the most opportunity for growth.

Maybe he would be the one.

They shared a passion for health and fitness, and their first days together were idyllic. They rode bikes to the beach, worked out together, and cooked wonderful meals. Lynda wasn't too concerned about the fact that Wade had been married three times before. He filled their conversation with Coast Guard stories, his youth, and about the bad choices he'd made with women. Her heart went out to him. After all, she was no stranger to making bad choices in romance. She thought of her first marriage and some of the failed relationships afterwards. Things happened. People grew and changed.

But some didn't.

The first incident occurred only two weeks after they started dating. They'd taken Wade's disabled father on a mini-vacation to a backwoods property thirty miles south of Lake City, a small town near the border of Georgia and Florida. The site of an old Seminole village, the town was originally called "Alligator Village." As she recalled the old name, she couldn't help but smile. She remembered reading that some mayor's wife refused to hang her lace stockings in a town called "Alligator", so they changed the name to Lake City.

The property had a trailer and a separate one-room cabin. After settling Wade's dad in the trailer and seeing him to bed, they'd planned to enjoy a perfect, romantic evening in the country. After all, they were still in the heady, first weeks of romance. And Wade had organized every detail, from the crackling fire to the red wine, from the stars to the moist Cuban cigars. While he built the fire, Lynda excused herself to freshen up in the cabin. Noticing they hadn't yet blown up their air mattress, she began readying it to save time later. That's when she accidentally dropped the air pump.

The sound of the pump hitting the floor startled Wade, who thought something was wrong with his dad. In a panic, he rushed into his dad's trailer. Seeing his father sleeping soundly, he bolted to the cabin where Lynda was, incensed.

"What the hell are you doing!" he yelled at her, still holding his cigar. Lynda watched its ashy smoke snake along the cabin's low roof. "Did I ask you to blow the mattress up yet?" Lynda scrambled to understand what was happening. Stunned, she tried to explain herself. But he ignored her explanations yelling, "You've ruined everything!" before slamming the door behind him and leaving her alone.

When she chased after him, she found him snuffing his cigar out. Then he stalked to their night picnic spot and snatched up the blankets and wine. He continued to insist that she'd ruined the whole evening while she reeled, still trying to gauge what she'd done wrong. The back-and-forth finally concluded when he tripped on a rock, stumbled towards the fire, and smothered it with a bucket of dirt. After they went to bed, her tears flipped to anger, and she turned her back on him in silence.

The next morning dawned with eggs, his meek apologies, and excuses she didn't care to hear. Confused and wanting to put the incident behind them, she accepted.

She didn't know then that this would become their pattern.

Spend a month or two – more if she was lucky – building up their world so he could tear it all down in an unprovoked rage. She justified his outbursts and abuse by believing they weren't really him, only his responses to unfortunate or difficult situations. The fact that he was still the same sweet, funny guy most of the time made her rationale easy, reasonable even. She just knew that if she could support him in changing the situations that made him unhappy, the outbursts would stop. But they never did. They only got worse.

He got into more debt. Employment was short-lived and unstable. He gained more and more weight. He got more depressed and angry. And he leaned more and more on Lynda.

By the time they eloped, she was effectively his lover, wife, business investor and landlord. Still, she loved him and believed that, even if he wasn't the perfect match, he fulfilled most of what she wanted in a partner. She so wanted it to work.

They both did.

But planning the big wedding ceremony brought all their unresolved conflict to a head. Wade wanted a big gala-style wedding, even though he couldn't pay for it. Lynda struggled to make him understand that her parents had already paid for her first wedding, and because of that, they wouldn't be footing the bill for this one. He became entitled and intractable.

The more she tried to persuade him that an intimate, backyard wedding was all she needed, the more he pushed for a high-dollar ceremony. And she wasn't sure how, but somewhere along the way, she ended up in the position of both planning and paying for it. Then Myrna died.

Under all this pressure, it didn't take long for her to realize that she felt exactly the same way she had as a child, constantly trying to appease someone who did nothing but criticize and invalidate her. Frighten her, even. As a child that person had been her mom. Now, it was Wade.

How had she allowed herself to fall into this pattern again?

CHAPTER ELEVEN
WILD ACRES

When Solly's wife died, his despair was all consuming.

And even though he never talked about God much, when she died, he observed the religious traditions completely. They seemed to be the measure of his love. The week before her burial, Solly's ears received the customary blessings, his soul the ritual consolations, his body the ceremonial foods. In his home, he placed a dark sheet over each mirror. He refrained from bathing or showering, and he grew his beard.

For days, he sat Shiva, his heart brought as low as the sawed-off stool he sat on. Then months went by. And he continued to shun joyful activities and pleasure. The world would try and fail to beckon him back out. Parties and celebrations were gruffly avoided. Concerts passed unattended. His sadness bled into year after year, as if all the light had left his life, never to return.

Mel never understood it. To him, it looked like giving up.

When Myrna died, he didn't want to give up on life. He wanted to celebrate her, everything he'd had with her. And he wanted to thrive beyond the grief that bore down on him like a tremendous wave. So when he sat on Mitch's floor to plan Myrna's funeral with the kids, it wasn't with a heart laid permanently low. And when his daughter-in-law suggested a Hawaiian theme for Myrna's Celebration of Life, he voted yes along with everyone else. Myrna had always loved Hawaii's dramatic beauty and traditional spirit of *aloha*.

The day of the Celebration, Mel was greeted by a riotous sea of Hawaiian shirts and dresses when he entered Mitch's home, carrying boxes of leis strung with orchids. Everyone in the family had contributed to the day. Melanie wrote the eulogy. Mitch wanted to keep at least one traditional custom, so funeral guests would be invited to shovel dirt on the coffin. Mark, the only one who couldn't make it in time to say goodbye to his mother, beheld her for the last time at a private viewing. The leis were Mel's idea.

Between family, friends, and the RYL community, so many guests packed the funeral home that they had to open an over-flow room and pipe in the service through speakers. Rows of chairs, pressed to the back wall, were full. Melanie delivered the eulogy, and Cindy spoke movingly about how important Myrna had been to the RYL community. Both of them, along with most of the guests, brightened the hall with their vivacious Hawaiian prints, creating a surreal, cheerful sight.

Mel was beyond grateful for this tiny mercy on this very sad day in his life.

Later in the afternoon, he was sitting beside Mitch in the procession when Mitch leaned over, pointing at the long line of cars stretching behind them. The procession was so long, it extended as far as they could see, and police were direct-ing traffic at intersections. Even though Mel wasn't the least bit surprised, he was still impressed. Throughout her illness, Myrna had always said she wanted all the prayers and energy she could get.

They were all still here.

Mitch must've been thinking similarly when he commented, "This is how powerful Myrna is, dad. She's holding up traffic." Mitch called his mom Myrna, just like Melanie often called

Mel, Melvyn. Mel nodded in agreement as the smell of orchids lingered in the backseat.

It clung to him long after he gently laid his lei on Myrna's coffin and said his final goodbye.

Lynda, still in shock, watched Myrna's funeral from the back row.

The room was over-crowded, and in the press of bodies, she fanned herself with her program. She felt irritated because Wade had made them late – again. She also felt helpless. She considered both Myrna and Mel among her closest friends, but she felt disconnected now.

On Carol's request, Lynda had stayed away because she believed that would be most helpful to Mel and his family. But now, even as she cried quiet tears, she felt a little detached, excluded.

She did manage to catch Mel on the steps outside the funeral home, where she hugged him and offered her condolences. His face appeared drawn and weary. She couldn't imagine what it was like to lose your life partner after almost fifty years together. Mel and Myrna had been the ideal for what so many people, including herself, wanted in a relationship. Now, she was faced with the stark reality that eventually, loss was part of that package.

Pursue your dreams and live life to the fullest because we never know how much time we have left.

And nothing brought this home like the death of a cherished friend.

She looked over at Wade. How much time did she have left and what did she really want for herself going forward? And, was it with him?

CHAPTER TWELVE

ONLY THIS SILENCE

"Hey Melvyn, where is the wine?" Melanie and Myrna's sisters were warming up the bar, and she headed off to grab a few bottles. Nearby, Joshie cooed from his dad's arms. Mel squeezed Joshie's plump fingers in his and scooped the baby into his arms. He was still waiting for most of the guests to arrive at Mitch's house for the *Celebration of Myrna's Life*.

Mel glanced around the room at some of their closest friends and family, then rested his gaze on Joshie's gummy smile. He realized how grateful he felt for each of them, these people who had surrounded him and Myrna throughout the years. He also, perhaps for the first time in many months, felt a sense of relief. For a year and half, he'd been powerless to help Myrna. Now, both of their suffering was finally over. She'd gone home.

He thought about all the grief work he'd done with people over the years. Now it was his turn. He hoped that work would hold him in good stead when he needed it most.

As if reminding himself, he exclaimed to Joshie, "We're here to celebrate *Bubbi*!" His voice was almost gleeful as he voiced the Yiddish word for *grandma* to the baby. Then, he spotted his cellphone sitting abandoned across the room and realized he hadn't checked it since leaving for the service. Shifting Joshie to one arm, he grabbed the phone off the side table, and was delighted to hear his friend Vickie's warm voice. Vickie was an RYL instructor who always seemed to have an upbeat, warm energy he and Myrna appreciated. He knew she was calling to pay respects from Aspen, but her message also contained a surprising story.

Apparently, she and her daughter were at a ski lodge in Aspen when they noticed something odd. They'd gone inside to adjust their lift ticket, and the clerk was wearing a short-sleeved Hawaiian shirt. This, in early March, one of the most frigid months in Colorado and in the midst of guests just like Vicky, clunking around in padded ski attire dusted with snow. Then Vicky had looked around and noticed that all the staff were wearing bright Hawaiian shirts, from the ski instructors to the cafe attendants to the rental clerks. When she asked why they were all wearing Hawaiian shirts in March, he shrugged. *An email came down from Corporate*, he said. *We were told to wear Hawaiian shirts today.*

When her message ended, he slid his phone in his pocket, oddly comforted but also intrigued. Myrna was well known for her ability to wield a quiet power. More than anyone, he especially held this opinion. But on this day, that power really seemed to be making itself known. Mitch's comments in the car. Now, here was Vickie's story. They lingered in the back of his mind as he received and mixed in with his guests.

Ever since his own mother had died from gallbladder cancer, he'd believed that souls survived death. Back then, he was still the Iceman so even though he felt sadness, he didn't cry. The day she died, his cousins came to the house. Mel's cousin asked him what time his mom had died. Mel thought it was a weird question but told him what he knew anyway. *The Coroner's report would say four AM.* At that, his cousin shared a story about how he woke up at four AM that morning and saw something he couldn't believe.

He described watching a scene form on the wall opposite his bed. In the scene, Mel's mother was sitting on a park bench with a beautiful lake stretching behind her. She held out her hand, offering a sugar donut to Mel's cousin, who was only two or three years old in the vision.

When Mel heard this story, he was intrigued and wondered if his mom was sending some kind of message. Later, as he sorted through pictures for her funeral, he found his answer.

There was a photograph of her sitting on a park bench at a lake. She was giving Mel's cousin a sugar donut.

Obviously, he reasoned, his cousin had re-experienced this repressed memory as some kind of dream. But what neither of them could ever explain is why it happened at the same time Mel's mother died.

Now, he was starting to feel the same precognitive sense that he had felt then.

Melanie interrupted his reverie and refilled his glass. "Need me to take him off your hands, Dad?" she asked, referring to Joshie. Mel declined, still preferring to circulate the room with the baby. The rest of the afternoon was pleasant, with people floating in and out of Mitch's, forming and reforming different circles. In general, everyone kept the atmosphere festive and light. It was what they all needed. Mel eventually forgot about Vickie's story until another interesting tale found him.

"Mel, I've *got* to tell you something," John, one of his friends said as he made a beeline for Mel. Mel, still in shock from the last few days, felt a little like the eye of a storm, calm but unnaturally so. He'd given the baby back to Melanie, so he kept his hands in his pockets as the circle he'd been talking to leaned in with interest.

"I'm listening," Mel replied eagerly. As soon as he heard his friend say, "It was the strangest thing," he knew it was about Myrna.

"A few days ago, I got in my car and my GPS suddenly came on. Now, I hadn't turned it on. It just came on by itself. I thought it was a misfire or glitch – until today when I was driving in the procession. When I took the road to the cemetery, I noticed the street sign said Wild Acres Road." His friend stopped to catch his breath for a moment and pause for effect. "That was the exact same road my GPS gave me directions to when it turned on earlier this week. I couldn't believe it!" Hearing this, Mel's back-of-mind reverie returned and intensified to sensation, an unmistakable zing of precognition buzzing under his skin.

Myrna's presence began to feel more and more possible.

"Isn't that interesting? Seems Myrna is busy today," Mel quipped. "Isn't that interesting" was one of his trademark phrases. It's how he often redirected himself or others to stay curious and open. But sometimes he said it just because something was, in fact, interesting. They all laughed and joined in with Myrna stories of their own, all of which occurred before she died. Except one from Myrna's brother.

"Remember the four phone calls on my cell at the funeral home?" he asked rhetorically. "Every time I answered, silence." Howard, her brother, gestured to the group and continued. "And no phone number. I'm telling you, it was my sister." After all the Myrna stories of the day, Mel had to agree. There were too many things science wasn't sophisticated enough to prove yet. Yesterday's impossibilities became present day realities all the time. Maybe this would be one of them. And, he thought, if anyone could pull it off, it would be Myrna.

The evening ended late, with about twenty close friends and family consoling one another with more stories and drinking wine until it was time to leave. Mel said his goodbyes, fielded final good wishes and hugs, and departed for the Loft. In the solitude of his car, the spiritual, even paranormal, tone of the day rose like a flame, then concentrated down to an essential, blue heart. It danced with the part of him that longed to hold on and let go at the same time. It made him, for a few brief moments, feel curious and hopeful. He wondered, if all *that* was indeed Myrna, if she was trying to let it be known that something of her still existed, something beyond the body she left behind.

He pondered this question for most of the drive home, but by the time he stepped up into the Loft, fatigue and grief had scattered his focus. He flipped on the light and set his personal effects on the tiny dinette table. The sheer routine of it was confronting and unreal, as if the world hadn't changed because Myrna was no longer in it. Each action he took was slow and deliberate, and suddenly took on the subtle pallor of sense-lessness, that of a tree falling in a forest with no one to hear.

Or, maybe it was just shock.

After all the activity of the day, all the people, all the stories, the Loft's silence was welcoming but also overwhelming. He was *alone*. He opened the refrigerator and pulled out a drink just to make a sound. Then he sat on the sofa and felt himself engulfed by a stillness far more profound than any tale of life after death.

He thought of all the people who'd surrounded him over the past week. Friends, family, his RYL community, neighbors, his kids, the grandkids. People he and Myrna had known and loved for decades.

Now, there was only the silence.

Myrna was gone.

But he was still here. There had to be some reason. What was it?

CHAPTER THIRTEEN
LIST NO.1

During the days after the funeral, Mel stayed close to the Loft.

He felt normal one minute, then the numbness and disorientation would descend. He sat on the couch to watch a ballgame only to awaken from intense flashbacks, cherished memories replaying in his mind. He talked to himself a lot, voices from the past intermingling with those of the current day with equal vividness. There were moments in which he was struck with tearful bouts of grief, sudden as a Florida storm on a summer afternoon. Perhaps what disoriented him most were the startling moments of clarity in which he'd find himself pondering all he'd been through, not only the last year and a half, but the entirety of his life. They would give rise to the most inexplicable, tender, and heartbreaking sense of appreciation. And he would find himself just standing there, crying tears of gratitude.

Friends called to check on him, and he appreciated the conversations. But then he'd be alone again, without the busyness of the past week's events to distract or comfort him. He was thankful he'd decided to go ahead and teach the upcoming RYL course. Teaching gave Mel something to focus on and to look forward to. The course had never been just about the students. It was his personal oasis, an opportunity to immerse himself in the RYL principles and to process his own life through the mirror of others.

He'd always loved being in the course room, but now, the sense of familiarity and community's support were a welcome refuge. Life outside the course room felt surreal.

He became his own student, applying the teachings he shared with others to help him through. Over the years, he'd seen many people struggle with managing and moving through their grief. His own understanding of it was anchored in knowing the difference between grieving and mourning. Grieving comprised all the necessary emotions of digesting loss. Mourning was getting stuck in grief. He witnessed his own father mourning the loss of Mel's mother for nearly 30 years. He promised himself he would not succumb to the trap of mourning.

Nights in the Loft proved to be the most challenging.

The sadness would peak sometime before bed, often delivering him dreamlessly to a bleak sensation of dread in the morning. He practiced honoring his feelings and then letting them go, and he'd find himself asking the same question again and again. *Myrna is gone. Why am I still here?*

This wasn't a question of blame or guilt. It was a searcher's question, a question of purpose. Why was he still alive and how would he discover the answer? This question was one of the things that excited him, gave him hope. He often revisited his belief that people are here to teach and to learn, and when they are finished, they get to leave.

A precocious, sixteen-year old girl named Becca had taught him this.

Becca was a grad and her father was an instructor. One day after she came home from school, she said to her mom, *I believe that we're here to teach and to learn, and when we're done, we leave.* She had been thinking about it, her mom supposed.

Two weeks after she shared her epiphany with her mom, she was killed in a car accident.

It was too late to ask now, but maybe this was Becca's answer to the meaning of life, and if it was, it was remarkably fierce in its truth. It was one of those truths that fascinated Mel because it came from someone so young, and it was so deceptively simple. He didn't realize how strongly it would reverberate through the years and teach him so very much.

Mel never forgot the night he visited her grieving parents.

He spoke with them before stepping into her bedroom to say a private goodbye. As he sat on her bed in the pillowed dark, he considered what he'd always regard as her last words.

We're here to learn and to teach. And when we're done, we get to leave.

The rightness of them overwhelmed him. She'd arrived with such a shining old soul. She taught. And when she was done teaching, she left. He remembered holding one of her favorite stuffed bears and turning it in his hands. It was threadbare in places, one of its eyes wobbling from a sewed hollow. Mel thought, *if Becca is right, and she was done learning and teaching, why am I still here?*

Years after sitting on that bed, after the death of his own wife, he was still Becca's student.

What did he have to teach and to learn? What would his new path be?

His first inkling came about a month after Myrna died, when he visited his son Mark out in Colorado.

Mark had a difficult time with his mom's death, especially since he hadn't been able to say goodbye before she died. His upcoming concert with the Gay Men's Chorus of Denver gave Mel an opportunity to support him. Myrna had made a promise to be there, and although it would never be the same without her, Mel wanted to fulfill that promise. His hope was that it would be a healing experience for them both.

The scale of the choral concert was accomplished and impressive, with over a hundred men giving a moving performance in a beautiful church. Mel knew Mark didn't get his musical talent from his dad, and it made him all the more proud, especially given what his son had been through. Mark showed his support too. One night after dinner, he leaned in and asked how Mel was doing. Mel had experienced such a whirlwind of emotions, it took a moment to know what to say.

"Well, everything is new and different," he finally said. It was an intentionally understated response, but nevertheless true. Though he'd experienced some of the most difficult feelings of his life, his son already knew that. They were in it together. And, Mel had long had a habit of being very intentional with language, so he was careful to avoid describing life or experiences as hard or difficult. These words carry a *heaviness* that affects our energy and can keep us stuck. He wanted to stay open, to be able to experience all the various feelings life was handing him, at once. "This was my first trip without your mom, and it's teaching me to learn new habits, like how to be alone . . . I'm growing." Then Mark asked something that caught him off guard.

"Do you think you might want another partner?" It was a big question Mel hadn't thought about yet. Was he ready to answer it now?

"Son, I guess if Upper Management wants me in a relationship, I'm open to it." He knew the moment he said it, it was the truth, and he felt proud of himself for expressing it.

On his return trip to Tampa, he started reading a book that explained how the universe, or Upper Management as Mel called it, supported creating the life people desired. *But you have to ask for exactly what you want*, the book argued. It encouraged him to ask himself what he wanted going forward. He thought back to his conversation with Mark. He'd always believed that having a partner was important in his life, and he probably didn't want to be alone forever. But it was also true that if wasn't meant for him to be in another relationship, he wouldn't force it.

He took out a legal pad and a pen. Then, he made a long wish list of all the attributes he'd like in a partner. He thought about what he loved about Myrna, and it flowed out so quickly that it startled him. When he sat back and read it, he realized that Myrna had possessed most of the qualities on the list. But there were a few new ones, too.

He looked at his list, not quite sure what to do with it. Then, he folded it slowly, put it in his planner, rested his head back, and dozed off.

Mel's Ideal Partner list

CHAPTER FOURTEEN

SLAMMED DOORS

The day after Mel arrived back in Tampa, Wade stopped by Lynda's house to sort through wedding details. It was early April, only a month before their big ceremony.

Brandy and Billy were at school and she'd just finished lunch. Because of his violent allergies to her cat, she and Wade had become accustomed to standing together in the entryway, taking care of minor business, and making plans to meet up somewhere else later. They were standing there when Lynda expressed how stressed she was that he was asking her to host a party for his friends while she was in the midst of planning their wedding. She didn't see how she could do it. He criticized her when she needed support – once again invalidating her feelings and expecting her to shoulder the bulk of the responsibility. Even though this had become their routine, she felt anger begin to rise within her.

Something shifted. She felt a new resolve root deep in her belly, and her anger began to boil over. Looking into his blue eyes left her cold.

The door was cracked open and her air conditioner switched on, humming in the background. Then she suddenly heard herself say, "I don't want to do this anymore." She hadn't planned to say it. It just came out. He hesitated.

"What do you mean?" Again, another answer came tumbling out. It had been true for quite some time.

"I don't want to be married . . . *to you.*"

Wade's eyes filled with venom. "That's really mean, Lynda!" She shook her head, adamant. He wanted her to be more concerned about his feelings than the truth. He wanted her to keep pretending.

"Well, it's the way I feel."

Wade lingered, seeming to size her up, then left suddenly, slamming the front door behind him. They had slammed so many doors in the course of their three-year relationship that he probably thought this was just another episode in their melodrama of conflict and rage. But as she stared at the door, she knew he was wrong.

It would be the last time.

The next few weeks in therapy showed her there would be no salvaging the relationship. The more she examined it, the more questions she asked herself, the clearer she became.

During one session, their therapist pointed out that she was in love with Wade's potential, something that was as unfair to him as it was to her. When the therapist asked her if she could love Wade just the way he was *and* be happy, she knew her answer would erase the last vestiges of her denial.

Yes, she could love him, but no, she could never be happy.

The relationship and everything she thought it meant, everything she had always wished it could be, melted in the clarifying heat of that truth.

CHAPTER FIFTEEN
EMERGENCE

Mel used his t-shirt to wipe sweat from his brow as he crouched to pin the towing bracket to the front of his car. It had been a month since he returned from his visit with Mark. He regarded the safety cables and tools littering the hot pavement at his feet, and his heart flooded with emotion. For a moment, he struggled to remember how he'd arrived at this moment. Why was he getting ready to climb into the Loft and head out on the open road *alone*? It was just one year ago that he and Myrna began their road trip together.

Traveling in the Loft had been their dream, her dream. Not his. What did he think he was doing?

Outwardly, the past month had been a relatively uneventful blur, a string of days that joined to form the second month without Myrna. He had taught RYL and found comfort in his friends and students. When he was asked, he heard himself telling people that things were okay, new, different. Sometimes, he thought about the list he'd made on the airplane. He still wondered about a new path, and he had faith that he'd find it. He'd been thinking about this when he'd heard a resounding inner voice, a knowing.

Take the motorhome out on your own. Just get back on the road.

Maybe it had been the grief, or the uncertainty of not knowing what would come next, or just the need to get out and move. Maybe it had been a memo from Upper Management. Maybe he just needed time, distance. He didn't care. The next day he'd woken up and started preparing to leave.

He didn't know where he would go, when he'd be back, or what he'd do. But he'd figure it out. He always had. The thought of the trip made him feel excited, scared, sad, often all at the same time. Sometimes moments of numbing shock would settle over him. But none of this emotional juggling had prepared him for the shell shock of actually driving away in the Loft without Myrna.

It almost felt worse than burying her.

The first three days on the road, he could not stop crying. Once or twice, he even had to pull off the road. But he didn't turn around.

He knew that the only difference between bravery and stupidity was the end result. To an outsider, his sudden departure so soon after his Myrna's death may have looked counter-intuitive, reckless even. Perhaps some felt that he should stay close to his work and community in his time of need. But he needed something altogether different. He didn't even know what it was. Grace, as he'd learned long ago and continued to learn, claimed no home address. He never found it. If he was lucky, if he was open, it would find him, no matter where he was. His inner voice had told him to go. *Go.*

First, he drove north to Tallahassee. He felt disoriented. He and Myrna had shared a hundred rituals and routines while on the road, and he'd never thought much about them until they were gone. And their time traveling in the Loft had been about her, her last trip. Now, it was about him. He had to figure things out by himself, decide the best route, when to stop, where to eat, when it was wise to get off the road or to keep driving.

After Tallahassee, he headed northwest to one of his favorite towns, New Orleans. Maybe it was the French heritage it shared with Montreal, his hometown. Or maybe, like many others, he was drawn to the invisible energy of humanity that coursed down Bourbon Street, with all its hidden stories. But this visit, something else riveted him to the core – the aftermath of Hurricane Katrina.

Though he'd seen it all unfold on the news, nothing could've prepared him for the sunken, dying city Katrina left in its wake, having landed only a few months before his visit.

With a friend who lived in the local area, he toured some of the worst parts of the damage. At some point, Mel shifted from tourist to witness, tucking his camera away and surveying the homes, flattened right on their foundations or blown completely away, never to be found. It was a land beyond sorrow.

Whole lives, entire families, the lustrous soul of the city diminished and broken in what was nothing less than a death. At certain poignant moments, he wondered if he'd made a mistake – if coming to New Orleans now of all times wasn't good for his state of mind.

But New Orleans was also still a city of wonder. And as he walked through the French Quarter on his last night in the city, he was reminded of this. He was taking an after-dinner walk through the Quarter when he noticed that somehow the people still found reason to celebrate. They were battered and bruised perhaps, but very much alive, and glad of it. At one point, he stopped to get his bearings and a man erupted in song,

Do you know what it means to miss New Orleans,
and there is something more,
I miss the one I care for even more
than I miss New Orleans. . .

Mel recognized the classic Louis Armstrong tune and quickly spotted the singer on a festooned balcony. A mild gust ruffled its bright garlands and flags just as the man ended his tune, emitting a deep belly laugh and taking an exultantly long draft from a large cocktail.

And that's when Mel realized it.

Yes, they were all here, still singing, still laughing, still celebrating *life*. The lesson lay in the contrast. These people were celebrating being alive precisely because they had experienced, were experiencing, so much darkness. He couldn't imagine the horror they had been through, but he also knew they were all trying to survive, just like he was. He felt something emerging inside him, something invisible and potent carried along by the busker's silky melodies and the jazz notes that floated from the endless line of bars and shops. It was almost unrecognizable, almost nameless.

Then he understood. It was hope.

Not only were they all still here, but he was with them, standing on a lively street corner in a city he'd always loved.

Both he and Myrna had believed everything happened for a purpose, that some kind of order reigned amidst chaos. And it was there, on the corner of Rue Dauphine and Rue St. Louis under the first stars of a falling dusk, that he felt his own purpose, his Passion, revive. Inexplicably, a crystalline sense of excitement and possibility broke like an unimaginably rogue, wild wave. There was no more room left for doubt or despair. No more time. The grief had finally pushed him through all that into the future, where there was more to do, more to experience and be. He knew he was forever changed by being with and losing Myrna. But he was still here.

There was another path and purpose waiting. He'd have to trust the process, as he often told students, and let whatever it was unfold.

CHAPTER SIXTEEN
TRUSTING THE PROCESS

On the road, *trusting the process* actually came easier than he thought it would. Maybe it was because the Iceman had thawed long ago. And Myrna's illness taught him how to live day by day, doctor appointment by doctor appointment, prayer by prayer.

New Orleans had been a door. But it was his time practicing living in the moment that gave him the strength to take his first steps. He finally began to experience the better side of "new and different." It emerged against the backdrop of the landscapes he traveled, and in the awe they inspired.

It was in the russet, sandstone canyons of Oklahoma where he meandered spellbound as the canyon morphed into the final destination for millions of stars. Stars he'd never forget. It was in New Mexico's stunning adobe horizons as he drove out of the dust of the Texas panhandle. And it was in the Vietnam War Memorial in Angel Fire, New Mexico.

Built by a couple who'd lost their twenty-one-year-old son to the war, the memorial was the first of its kind – a place to honor and remember. The memorial's hushed media room looked almost like a church with its rows of benches that invited visitors to sit and watch the film *Letters Home*. Several large tissue boxes were placed along each bench.

After he watched the film he understood why.

Utterly transported, he cried through the entire film, grieving for the lost.

Each tear felt purifying, like the kind that empties the soul and cleanses the spirit. And they continued long after the film was over. Finally, he grabbed a handful of tissues, stepped outside, and called a friend who'd served in Vietnam. "Thank you," Mel said into the phone. "I'm so proud of you." His gratitude contained the grief he felt for the kids who'd never had a choice, who'd been drafted into the war only to survive and return to a nation in turmoil. Or, to never come home at all. As he mulled over their plight, he wondered if it was possible for them to ever really return home.

And he knew he was also crying for himself. For him, home had changed irrevocably. Perhaps he also wondered, half-consciously, if it was possible for him to ever return home.

While he now felt free, Myrna had been his rock. She had been home. Without her, where would home be? What would it mean?

After Angel Fire, Mel headed to Colorado to visit Mark again. And at the end of June, he flew back home to teach RYL. He didn't know it, but his new path was getting ready to reveal itself. And he would soon learn what he was willing to give up for joy, for love, for purpose . . . and for Passion.

CHAPTER SEVENTEEN
THINGS THAT HAPPEN

It felt electric.

When Mel walked into the Suncoast Girl Scouts Building to teach RYL, it always did. The volunteer graduates, called *assistants*, were happy to see him, and greeted him warmly. Many of them felt as excited as he did to be back in the course room. It's what had changed and continued to change their lives.

When it was time to teach a course, Mel's top priority was serving the students. Even though he'd traveled for an entire month by himself, he'd still devoted considerable time to planning, recruiting, and supporting students whenever they called. Sometimes he'd spend an hour or more helping a grad process through a personal issue. This was the kind of open-door policy with which Myrna took issue.

He'd interrupt dinner for a call and stay on as long as needed. He knew this practice had sometimes made his kids feel as if they came last, too. He didn't know if he was right or wrong, but he believed coaching was fundamental to the integrity of his work. He couldn't only be available to students in the course room. He wanted to be available when necessary.

Together, he and the assistants trucked in food and supplies and set up the course room with several rows of chairs, an easel and whiteboard, and two director chairs at the front. The final touch was dimming the room to a warm glow to create a feeling of security – like a favorite blanket. All the assistants were former RYL students, and some were also serving as "angels," which meant that they would perform the special task of mentoring and helping a new student throughout the weekend.

Assistants participated in the entire weekend, witnessing each student's processing and often deepening their own personal growth as a result. This model of sharing, witnessing, and extreme vulnerability was a heightened embodiment of the philosophies Mel had learned – that the best of teaching and learning often occurred at the same time. Staying present, open, and humble to them was the real work, and this was what led to transformation.

The June course had eight students and twenty-six assistants. It also included generations of families, something Mel always found very special. Gerry, her daughter Suzy, and Suzy's teenage son Nick, would be participating as assistants. Suzy's son Alex was a student. Then there was also Lynda.

She would be assisting, while her son Billy was a student. Billy and Alex also brought something besides family connection – the unique perspectives and presence of teenage boys. Mel had made sure to speak with each boy individually before the course, and he clarified the issues each wanted to address over the weekend. And Lynda had been concerned about Billy because he'd recently dropped out of high school and had no plan. He was drifting.

All the assistants and students were settled in their chairs when he and Cindy entered the course room and sat in their director chairs. After introductions and meeting everybody in the room, he took a deep breath and began.

"Ninety percent of what is imprinted in the minds of adults come from childhood. As children, we observe an experience, we make decisions and interpretations, and without the skills and tools to process it, it gets buried in our subconscious.

Therefore, the beliefs that run our adult lives were created by decisions we made as children."

Mel paused and read the room. He scanned the students who sat in the front row and the assistants seated behind them to see who was being triggered by what was being shared. "Obviously, this can cause problems," he joked dryly. Knowing chuckles ripped through the room, as well as a tear or two. He continued. "We think the events that happened *to* us cause us pain. But it's what we chose to make these events *mean* – the beliefs we created – that actually cause us pain." He and Cindy sat silently to let the idea sink in. Then she picked up and explained how belief-based decisions were based on five areas: men, women, relationships, life, and self.

"These are the areas we'll go back to and look at," she said. "And what I want each of you to remember is that, no matter what you brought into this room to change, or how over-whelmed you may feel, when you change your mind about your story, you begin to change your life." Mel nodded in agreement.

"Throughout the weekend, we'll pause to check in and give you an opportunity to express how you're feeling." he added. "Would anyone like to share their thoughts or feelings so far? Any 'aha' moments?"

"Well, I really want to stop being so angry at my mother, but sometimes she says things that really hurt me," one student said hesitantly. Everyone seemed to hear the longing in her voice. All of them had felt it at some point in their lives. Some of them probably felt it now.

Mel stroked his beard with his thumb and first finger, deep in thought. "There are two things going on here. One is your mother's behavior, and the other is your *feelings* about your mother's behavior. You have no control over your mother's actions, but you have total control over yourself and how you choose to feel." The student nodded, and Mel continued. "Let me say it another way. If something is triggering you – pushing your buttons – it is much easier to disconnect the button than it is to change someone else. Does that make sense?"

The room grew quiet as people considered this. Heads nodded in assent. It seemed to say it all. Cindy took Mel's hand, a common gesture of friendship and teamwork that they often shared while teaching.

"So, with your courage and permission, this weekend we'll explore how to do it differently. Would you like that?" Mel asked, to a resounding "yes!"

"Then let's get started."

CHAPTER EIGHTEEN
INDEPENDENCE DAY

A few days later on July fourth, Mel hit I-275 and headed west from Tampa to Indian Rocks Beach. It was a beach he knew well, being right across Gulf Boulevard from his and Myrna's old townhouse. An RYL grad had organized an outing at the Pub for dinner, and at Indian Shores for fireworks afterwards. He flipped the windshield wipers on to clear the translucent glaze of moisture left behind from an earlier rain burst. Besides ushering in a welcome relief from the heat, the afternoon torrent also had the distinction of initiating the day's soft slide into cooler evening temperatures.

Mel could practically set his watch by the summer afternoon rainstorms of Florida. They blew out as fast as they blew in, and though the storm had ended only minutes ago, no sign of precipitation remained in the swath of clear, blue Tampa sky that spread out in every direction above him. Now, white wisps waiting to become tomorrow's storm floated in the sky. It was going to be a good – no, a great night for fireworks.

As he crossed the bridge across Old Tampa Bay, something Solly said recently drifted back to him. *Melvyn, you still living the gypsy life?* He thought of the Loft waiting back in Colorado.

He missed it. But as the vivid, blue, sparkling expanse of the Bay unfurled, its natural beauty stunned him, almost as if he were seeing it for the first time. Before he went out on the road, the routines of living in Tampa and grieving Myrna's death had dulled his appreciation of his surroundings. Now, its beauty felt strange and new, almost leaving him breathless.

It had only been four months since Myrna died, and so much had changed. He thought of his time in New Orleans... New Mexico... Colorado. He'd experienced a level of sadness more profound than any in his life, but incredibly, he'd also begun to experience a new kind of joy. It was as if grief had the power to infuse every moment with heightened meaning and color, with possibility, and with a kind of gratitude that perhaps only arises out of the deepest darkness. As he neared the Pub, he wondered if he appeared as changed as he was beginning to feel.

He pulled into a parking space and shook his head free of all these thoughts. *Myrna, you got to leave*, he thought as he pulled his keys out of the ignition, opened the car door, and swung his legs out. A small, downy grey feather settled by his shoe before skittering away. The air smelled salty and a little brackish. He looked up, watched a seagull wheel away. *But I'm still here. So what's next?*

As he strolled away, he remembered the beach rendezvous after dinner and returned to put his nose to the car's back window. He'd forgotten to bring beach chairs. He figured someone would bring extra.

They always did.

CHAPTER NINETEEN
OTHER SIDE OF LEAVING

"Wow, it's already so crowded!" Lynda exclaimed as she and her friend Gerry pulled into the Indian Shores Beach access and began scanning for a parking spot. They were just arriving from the July fourth RYL dinner at the Pub. Lynda felt a pang of sadness as she thought of all the times she'd pulled into this same access to attend one of Mel and Myrna's famous July fourth parties. Then she soothed herself with humor.

"Hey Gerry, if I use my intention, do you think I can manifest a spot like they do in *The Secret*?" Lynda had met Gerry, a warm southern woman in her seventies, years ago. And even though she was decades younger, Lynda enjoyed Gerry's company because she often offered a valuable perspective to life. Like Lynda's mom, Gerry married into south Tampa elite, but rather than being entitled, she was humble. Lynda loved that about her.

"Hon, I think you can manifest just about anything you want," Gerry replied. Then she pointed. "Hey, the kids are already here – there's Suzy's van." Brandy and Billy had gotten a ride from the restaurant with Suzie, Gerry's daughter.

"Okay, manifesting in 3 . . . 2 . . . 1 . . ." Lynda said as she squeezed her car into one of the few remaining spots. Like most jokes, it contained significant truth. Lynda was deeply spiritual and had come to believe that she could manifest what she desired. That's what much of her self-development and work in RYL had entailed. Rooted in her childhood, there was a part of her that believed she could never get what she wanted – that fulfillment was for other people, not her. She wanted to root this sense of unworthiness out, to know what it was like to reach her dreams and experience true happiness.

Gerry patted Lynda's knee. "Well, there you go," she said, referring to the nearly full parking lot. "Just like magic!" They both laughed as they got out and began gathering beach supplies.

Because she was raised in Tampa, going to the beach was a well-oiled routine. Lynda had learned to pack light and keep it simple. Keep basic beach supplies, extra towels, and a couple of chairs in the car at all times. Only park at beach accesses with a spigot or outdoor shower. Take your shoes off and put them in the car. Put on flip-flops. Double-check vehicle to see if there are any visible valuables inside. Ditto for sunscreen, hat, keys. Put sunshade in windshield, lock car up, and whatever you do, as she always reminded her kids Billy and Brandy, try not to put your shoes back on until all the sand is off your feet. Perhaps this penchant for organization came from her years managing and teaching fitness classes at the Y while being a single mom.

Gerry and Lynda chitchatted as they walked side by side onto the narrow path. Lynda absolutely loved the calm water of Florida's west coast. A bad storm could render the Gulf choppy, but it was a kiddy pool compared to the Atlantic. *And more beautiful*, Lynda thought as she emerged from the shade of palm trees, crested a wooden walkway, stepped onto the white sand, and took in the sun-swept panorama. Something about the ocean and the beach's beauty had always made her feel so happy and free. And on this day, she felt extra emotional for some reason. Maybe it was missing Myrna. Or, maybe it was that both her kids were now part of her RYL family, allowing her to feel even closer to them than she already did. She and

Billy had been through an especially challenging time, and for the first time in a while, she felt hopeful.

She squinted in the sun, spotting Brandy, Billy and their friend, Nick, loitering at the water's edge.

"There they are!" she exclaimed as she headed in their direction. The kids were too far away for her to see their faces, but as she walked, she watched their body language. Brandy stood close to Nick while Billy meandered towards the water. Brandy tilted her body towards Nick in a slight but telling movement. A gentle gust ruffled Brandy's thick, blonde hair, eliciting a self-conscious flick of her head. She's always had the most beautiful head of hair, Lynda thought as she continued to watch. The kids started laughing as Nick drew closer to Brandy.

Of course, Lynda thought, as she watched their dance of attraction unfold. Nick hurled a stick into the water as Brandy looked on attentively. Lynda couldn't deny the chemistry. Maybe that spark would grow into a flame. Lynda beamed, reveling in the fact that she'd played the role of matchmaker during this past weekend. She remembered the moment Nick saw Brandy for the first time after the assistant meeting.

The Wednesday night prior to a course was the FOAM – First and Only Assistant Meeting. Afterwards, as they were walking to their cars, Lynda mentioned that her daughter had attended RYL recently, and Nick was intrigued. So Lynda showed him a picture of Brandy. When he looked at the picture and exclaimed "Whoa!" Lynda offered to introduce them. She liked Nick and his family, and since Brandy would be attending the Sunday graduation ceremony to support her brother, she thought that would be a good time.

She'd waited to mention it to Brandy. She wanted Brandy to be in the same space as Nick for a while without being self-conscious, so she'd have time to form her own impression of him before Lynda said anything. This would also allow Lynda to gauge her response and get permission. And it was decisive. "Mom," Brandy gushed, "he's sooo cute." When Lynda introduced them a few moments later, Nick looked at Brandy and said, right in front of Lynda, "Hi, I'm Nick. I'm going to marry you one day."

"Well," she heard Gerry quip beside her, "Brandy and Nick are having a fine time of it." As Nick's grandmother, she must have also been feeling especially interested in the developing romance.

"I know – it's so sweet . . . I just love Nick."

It was hard for Lynda not to bask in their connection because it was also an RYL connection. She'd seen relationships blossom between fellow assistants in the past, and they were all unique, but this one was really special because it connected these two RYL families. And now, as RYL graduates, both Billy and Brandy were not only her kids but part of her beloved community. What more could she ask for?

She felt the sand tickle her feet as she tuned into her body. The beach hummed with laughter and the shrill pops of early fireworks. A wash of bliss came over her, the sounds around her melting together. She'd been through a lot with Wade recently, but it didn't seem to matter in this moment. She felt totally unburdened, grateful even, as if she'd survived something and come out on top. Maybe it was the afterglow of a tender and heartfelt weekend at RYL, or the love of family and friends, or the years of work to get to this point. Perhaps things weren't perfect, and perhaps she didn't have everything she wanted. But on this July fourth, she knew there were plenty of reasons to celebrate the personal independence and freedom she'd fought for.

A nearby boombox was playing a fun '80s tune, and Gerry and Lynda began to dance their way through the thick sand. "Hey Mom!" Suzy shouted and waved. "Over here." Laughing, the two women headed towards a small band of chairs where their friends had begun to assemble. Only a few people had arrived, but their numbers would grow through the evening as more made their way from their homes or the Pub. A few chairs sat abandoned by their owners as people milled around. Lynda spotted Billy's empty chair and planted hers down beside it.

A random line from a favorite country song played in her mind, *"Oh, you're on the feel-good side of leavin'."* She thought it was ironic. The only leaving she'd done lately was the hardest kind. And the best kind. As difficult as her relationship with Wade had been, she had to admit she was already on the feel-good side. The smooth side with no regrets or self-recriminations. The side where only one earnest question bobbed into her mind. *Why did it take me so long to realize I created a relationship just like the one I had with my mother?*

If she hadn't realized that she couldn't love Wade and be happy at the same time, he'd probably be sitting here in one of the empty beach chairs. Or, standing beside her, making her feel like she was tiptoeing on eggshells instead of warm, yielding sand. And there'd be one more difference. She glanced at her hand.

An engagement ring would be on her finger.

CHAPTER TWENTY
LIVING IN THIS MOMENT

"Lynda, you look like you're positively basking," Lynda's friend Deb said to her as Deb sat down. Lynda winked, appreciating that Deb had noticed something was different. Then she heard Carol a few feet away exclaiming that they'd be able to see the fireworks clear to St. Pete. She and Carol had been friends a long time, but Lynda felt a slight twinge as she watched Carol pick up a CD player, position herself under a palm tree some distance from their group, and start dancing and swaying her body, almost seductively. Carol had been the one who told her "family only" when Myrna was taken to hospice. Carol had sometimes seemed like she could be a little demanding at times, but that's also what made her good at other things, like her job, and getting good seats at the club. Lynda wasn't sure what the uneasiness in her gut was about, but she had learned to trust it. Something was off. Not wanting to let anything spoil her mood, Lynda shifted her focus as she sat down with Deb, Billy's chair sitting empty between them.

She stretched her legs, toned and shapely, out in front of her. Even though she was in her mid-forties, a lifetime of exercise and healthy living had kept her vibrant and youthful. Her fair, lightly freckled skin was clear, her red hair shiny, and her muscles strong and supple. Most of all, she was at ease in her own skin, a treasure she never took for granted. All through her childhood and teenage years, kids had made fun of her red hair and freckles and, of course, her mother's comments never helped matters. It had taken her a long time to appreciate her physical appearance.

She rifled through her beach bag for her sunglass case. Even though the after-dinner sun diminished on the horizon, its glare still demanded a little respect. She needed a moment to lay her head back and decompress between dinner and the evening's upcoming festivities. She ran her fingers through her chin-length hair, closed her eyes, and felt the sun's warmth fall on her face. She felt so content, and it was hard for her to believe she'd just ended a three-year relationship. And technically, it was also a six-month marriage, which made her response seem even more surreal.

A flurry of small fireworks jolted Lynda out of her reverie. She blinked her eyes open as the sunset turned the sky beautiful shades of pink and purple. Deb sat chatting with other RYL'ers, and she listened to her friends' conversation for a few moments as more RYL'ers trickled in, exchanged hugs, and set chairs up.

Refreshed and ready for the evening, Lynda sat up, flashing enthusiastic waves at newly arriving friends. Then, she saw Mel walking towards her without a chair of his own. She hadn't gotten a chance to connect with him during the weekend course, so she was excited to see how he was doing and how his travels were going.

"Hey Mel!" Lynda called to him as she patted the tops of her thighs and laughed.

Startled in the best possible way, Mel peered towards her to see who was calling his name. Getting the joke, he grinned, headed in her direction, and made as if he would do exactly that – sit right in her lap. At the very last second, she laughed, exclaiming, "No, no, you can have Billy's chair—he's off with the other teens by the water!" Mel heard Deb chuckle as he landed square in the chair between her and Lynda.

"Are you sure Billy won't be mad at me if I steal his chair?" Mel joked.

Lynda rolled her eyes playfully. He always teased her like a big brother. Then he asked more earnestly, "So, how are my kids, anyway?" He'd called Brandy and Billy "his kids" for years. Lynda nodded towards the water's edge, waiting to see if he'd discern the budding romance.

"Your kids are great, especially one of them," she remarked with a hint of irony. Mel smiled and regarded her and Deb, who both sported wind-blown hair, t-shirts, and jean shorts in typical Florida fashion. Deb wore a hot pink baseball cap while dark sunglasses veiled Lynda's eyes. A hint of mischief twinkled in his eyes.

"We want to hear all about where you've been and what you've been doing with yourself, Mr. World Traveler!" Deb exclaimed.

"Well, I'm more of a North American Continent Traveler," he replied, looking at Deb, then at Lynda. "So the kids," he said suggestively as he gestured towards Brandy and Nick, "they're enjoying the evening?"

"Mm-hmm," Lynda answered, not even trying to hide the enthusiasm in her voice. "They seem to be really into each other."

"Indeed," Mel replied approvingly. Then, his expression shifted, becoming more contemplative, even a little sad. "First love, eh?" he asked the women rhetorically. Then, Deb changed the subject.

"So, where did you fly in from this time, Mel?" Mel's words grew clear and pointed, as if he remembered every date, time, and place with perfect recall. "At the beginning of June, I drove from Florida to New Orleans and then into Memphis, Arkansas, Texas and New Mexico. Then I drove up to Golden, Colorado to see my son Mark, and that is where I flew from."

"Good grief, I can't keep up with you," Deb quipped.

"Yeah, that's quite a solo, Mel," Lynda added. Even if she didn't know what it was like to lose your life partner, she understood the need for solitude. "Tell us more about it."

"Oh, it was incredible. I've seen buskers and beads on Bourbon Street, canyons of Oklahoma, adobes of New Mexico, and the snow-capped mountains of Colorado – all in a month's time."

"So what was your favorite place?" Lynda asked, sipping her water.

"Well, I always enjoy seeing Mark . . . and as for favorites, I can't say. It was all wonderful." The trio paused to take in the ocean. "Just like I'm going to enjoy the fireworks on this beach," he said as he regarded the waves. "There's something about traveling. Helps me live in the moment, I guess, like I'm doing now." Indian Shores, sitting on a thin, finger-shaped peninsula with a canal running through it, held a tender place in his heart. On one side was the ocean and, a stone's throw away, the Intercoastal Waterway ran along the other side. He and Myrna's old townhouse was right across the road on the Intercoastal side, and because he'd spent years there, he still thought of Indian Shores as his own panorama backyard, full of barbecues and beach sunsets.

He stared into the last remains of the melting, orange sun. Pastel hues tinged with darkness and dusk gathered around it. He suddenly felt sad. "This is the first Fourth of July Myrna won't be with us," he said to his two friends. He said it plainly, a simple statement of fact, as if Myrna were at home taking a nap. Then he felt the moist, stinging sensation of salty tears rising. They left a passing mist in his eyes.

Sometimes, memories are a part of living in the moment.

CHAPTER TWENTY-ONE
GROUND ZERO

On one level, Lynda and Deb were aware that more of their friends were arriving but, just for now, it didn't matter. Each took one of Mel's hands in theirs. The emotional focus of the three narrowed, forming a shield around them as they continued their hushed conversation within their intimate bubble.

"I'm used to it, you know?" he said, referring to the tears. "They come out of nowhere, and then they leave. But I still feel happy much of the time. I've just started to feel happy again. The road trip, it was about Myrna . . . and myself. It went from sadness to 'life-goes-on' in three weeks." Then, he paused before adding playfully, "that must be a record." As Lynda listened to her friend's words, a protective response welled up within her, surprising her with its intensity.

"Makes sense," she said. "You've probably already done a lot of your grieving. The year and a half you took care of her, the funeral, the weeks after that . . . don't forget all that." She didn't believe grief needed to look any particular way or last a particular length of time. She also believed that actions and attitude would affect how quickly someone could move through grief. RYL's focus on a deeper connection with yourself and faith in a higher power backed this up.

As the three of them let Mel's comments simmer, movement in the corner of Lynda's eye distracted her. It was Carol. Still dancing, and Lynda wondered if she was trying to get attention. She recalled something Carol had said to her only a month ago, when Mel had met a female friend for lunch. "Mel shouldn't be dating." But lunching with people was nothing new. Mel met people all the time to talk about RYL and build relationships. Lynda had come to Mel's defense. So what if he was dating? The guy had gone through hell. How long does someone have to suffer before they're allowed to live again? She knew everyone had their own ways of dealing with grief. She respected Carol's opinion, but she didn't agree. Not at all.

Deb broke the group's silence. "It's actually not that strange. Most grief therapists say that around the third month after a death, people start feeling better."

"So, I'm right on time!" Mel retorted. They all laughed, but Lynda was aware of the tragedy lying just beneath his humor. Seagulls, excited by the prospect of left-behind potato chips and alarmed by the fireworks, shrieked over their heads. Then a few RYL'ers broached their bubble brandishing unlit sparklers.

"It's almost 9:00," one of them said, her companions shielding their lighters from the breeze. "Fireworks are starting!" Another offered a sparkler to Mel but he declined.

"No thank you, my dear, but I am looking forward to the fireworks." Just then, a loud stunner of purple sparks exploded in the dark sky. They all pivoted their faces up and gawked.

"Woo! That was a good one!" Lynda heard someone from a nearby group shout. Because she'd attended several of Mel and Myrna's July fourth parties at this beach, she knew the city fireworks would be too far off to notice much. The spectacle would come instead from private fireworks, like the one that just popped off. Their friends floated away with their lit sparklers, leaving a pretty trail of tiny white-hot sparks behind them.

As Mel surveyed the scene, he felt grateful for his friends and community, now swollen to a party of about thirty. Though many of their faces were shadowed, he recognized his friends' voices through the "ooh's and ah's" and other sounds of celebration. He felt even more grateful to be sitting with Lynda and Deb, holding their hands. Nothing to hide. Nothing to pretend. Just presence and warmth. Just being together. He knew he wasn't a perfect teacher or friend or even leader, but he shared a vision with all these people, and that vision had brought them all together, to this beach, to this moment.

Mel, Lynda, and Deb all settled back in their chairs, eyes turned upward for the show. They *oohed* and *aahed* as Roman candles shot off to the left, and whistlers and spinners rocketed off to the right. The sound of firecrackers and smoke filled the air. As they focused on the celebration in the sky, Mel noticed something odd, a strange sensation that jolted him from the atmosphere of community and friendship. Someone, either Deb or Lynda, was lightly brushing the side of his thumb with her thumb.

It was Lynda. She was the source of the nearly imperceptible back-and-forth caress.

Impossible, he thought, taken aback and a little embarrassed. *She's always been like my sister.* Then, despite himself, he felt the gooey blush of a high-school kid sweep across his cheeks, a development that embarrassed him even more. *Lynda's one of my best friends*, he reminded himself, hoping this would dampen the inexplicable force of hope blossoming within his body. *But*, the hope seemed to counter.

He was caught between two instincts, wanting to both chalk it all up to his imagination and pause to get more information. He decided to compare his hands to one another. With laser focus he felt into the place where Deb's hand made contact with his right hand. Nothing. It was a friend holding another friend's hand. Trying to look casual, he felt into it again. Still nothing. Then, he concentrated on the place where his left hand joined Lynda's. It was the unmistakable sensation and allure of skin to skin.

It was *everything*.

He tried to hide his growing sense of shock. Through all their years of friendship, he'd never felt any attraction for Lynda, and, as far as he knew, she'd never felt any for him. He recalled his list back at the Loft and his conversation with Mark. He'd opened himself up to a new relationship and maybe . . . someone was accepting the invitation. Even though it felt so remarkable and crazy and awkward, he didn't want to close down to whatever might come next.

Not knowing what to think or do, Mel fixed his gaze on the fireworks blooming in a spectacular parade of smoke and light. His left hand, now most definitely a ground zero of sensation, bewilderment, and adrenaline, trembled under their vibrations.

CHAPTER TWENTY-TWO
SPARK

DIY firework displays strung the beach with their chaotic, technicolor bursts, leaving haze and smoke in their wake. Lynda, lost in a delicious, light-induced trance, allowed herself to be lost in the display. Haphazard collections of blankets, beach umbrellas, towels, and chairs surrounded her, stretching as far as she could see, which wasn't far. Just ahead, three figures huddled in semi-shadow lighting a ground firework. They all leapt backwards as it sparked, firing a shocking pink arc skyward to scattered applause.

Its smoky discharge made her eyes water, and she blinked a few times as she surveyed the hazy flow of friends and strangers around her. The air was infused with the smell of fresh-lit matches. She lifted her water bottle to quench her thirst when she noticed a sensation in her right hand.

Her hand was still clasped with Mel's, her thumb gently moving across his thumb. Rather too intimately, she thought, as she stilled the movement.

Her eyes flickered to the sand as she marveled, a little in shock, at her hand's mysterious independence. She wondered if she should apologize or just pretend nothing happened. Slightly embarrassed, she decided to forget it. Mel was like a brother. If he noticed anything, he'd probably just assume she was being affectionate and think nothing of it. But just as she began to brush it off, Mel, or rather his hand, began to respond in kind, his thumb stirring its own rhythm in a tiny caress that was as impossible to ignore as it was to interpret. The unmistakable flutters of attraction that started to swirl in her belly plunged her deeper into confusion.

She rallied to reestablish her composure, glancing casually at Deb, who still held Mel's other hand. The beach was a mishmash of smoke, moonlight and electric fireworks, all of which combined to obscure her vision. It was impossible to determine if he was rubbing Deb's hand or not. If he was, Lynda could safely assume that nothing out of the ordinary was happening between them. After all, he was always physically affectionate with his friends, always had been. One of the first things she'd ever noticed about him were the deep, warm hugs he bestowed whenever he greeted any of his friends or family. That behavior was followed by reassuring shows of affection and familial intimacy. And it was also pretty standard in RYL, something that had always made her feel safe.

But the question lingered.

She couldn't help wondering if he was rubbing Deb's hand, too. *Was* this just another one of their friendly best-buddy gestures? To her it felt like something more. And very real. She'd always felt like he was family, and never felt any physical attraction for him, at least not consciously. She did recall one time at Myrna's and Mel's house when she'd looked at Mel and thought he was attractive for an older man. It was no more than a passing thought but now, she also remembered wondering what it was like to be Myrna.

Her body expanded its range of perception, his presence waxed, becoming more intense, more *there*. She took a deep breath, an attempt to release the anxious tension in her belly. After all, this event was probably silly, meaningless . . . with the exception of those flirty, internal butterflies. She shifted in her seat.

She'd always wondered why people called them butterflies. Butterflies were delicate and insubstantial, and far too whimsical to compare to the tectonic churning of physical, chemical attraction. Which, if it was happening to her, was probably happening *only* to her. Then again, she couldn't help but wonder if Mel was feeling something . . . what he was doing and *why*. After all, it was possible that – oh, she didn't know what was possible. That was the problem. She needed more information but resisted the temptation to look directly at him.

Resorting to the next best source of information, she panned for clues in their recent conversations. Had she overlooked something? They'd talked about the Wade drama a lot. And, to a lesser extent, they'd also discussed Mel's journey, how he was getting along after Myrna's death, where he was traveling, who he was with. Though she wasn't sure why, one particular conversation stood out. It occurred shortly after she canceled the wedding with Wade. She'd called Mel while he was on the road to tell him. After all, he was scheduled to officiate the big wedding ceremony.

She'd waited several weeks to tell him that she'd called it all off. She was afraid he'd be disappointed in her, or that he'd criticize her for giving up. She knew he believed that relationships are forever.

When she finally got the nerve to call him, she explained that she just realized that Wade always made lots of promises but never delivered, and she ended up carrying the load. Nothing had really changed in three years, and she just didn't want that to be the rest of her life. Mel's response was more of a statement than a question. "So," he'd said, "you decided not to settle." She'd felt surprised and relieved. He'd seen the mismatch all along but had been a good enough friend to support her and let her make the decision for herself.

She remembered how on that same call, the discussion had segued to life partners. He'd shared a story about reading a book called *Ask and It Is Given*, about the nature of the universe and the law of attraction. He'd told her all about how it had inspired him to make a list of what he wanted. The book was all about universal love and putting in your order for what you want in life. How Myrna was gone and that he still wanted a partner. His next words were perfectly preserved in her memory. "My hand simply wrote – I didn't even have to think about it. It's long and most of it comes from Myrna because I loved so many things about her. But, there were two or three things that were different."

Sitting here, she now felt a burning desire to know what those two or three things were. Had she even asked? She wasn't sure.

She did remember Mel suggesting that she find clarity around her own ideal partner – which Wade clearly wasn't – by making her own list. And that was what jarred her memory. She'd already made a long-forgotten list. It probably sat forlorn in a drawer under unopened junk mail and emergency flashlights. Or maybe it was crammed in the bottom of a missing picture box. But she knew she'd made one after her divorce from her first husband, years before her conversation with Mel, and misplaced it. As heartbroken and attached as she was to her first husband, she knew the list would help her move on. At the time, its existence gave her hope that she might one day find love again.

She believed in soul mates then. She always had. Finding a life-long love had always been one of her biggest dreams. And even though she didn't mention her list to Mel on the phone that day, she knew he was right about the list. She decided she had to find it.

After they ended their call, she found herself unsuccessfully rummaging for the list, finally suspending her fruitless search with a promise that she'd find and rewrite it as soon as she could. The prospect of revisiting it excited her. It took a week or so until she found it, faded on a limp piece of grungy notebook paper. She'd spent a couple days musing and updating it, and then wrote her new and improved list on a fresh piece of paper. Then she laid it carefully on her bedside table, a location she imagined as appropriately dream-soaked and auspicious for something as magical as a soul mate wish-list. It was sitting there now.

Before she could stop herself, she turned to look at Mel. As she did, he met and held her gaze, lifting his eyebrows in that bemused, question-mark of an expression she'd seen so many times, as if to say *isn't this interesting*. And she wasn't sure how, but she began to feel something like an amber, honey-like cord of energy flowing between them.

CHAPTER TWENTY-THREE
CONFESSIONS

Neither of them said anything.

The moon, high and near-full, cleared a swath of clouds, pouring light on the beach. Mel had been friends – great friends – with Lynda for years. But sitting here, she appeared completely different. Maybe it was the moonlight, but her skin looked creamy, almost luminescent. And her eyes, normally spirited and blue, appeared soulful and bottomless. In this moment, he realized how beautiful she was.

It felt like a revelation.

He noticed her brows knit together as she broke their gaze and looked out towards the dark waves. But she continued holding his hand. He became self-conscious, remembering Deb, and peeked over at her. Had she seen or sensed anything unusual? Was there anything unusual to see? Deb appeared happily distracted, and he hoped she was.

"Well, this is quite a show." Mel knew it was a little banal and kept his voice measured. Flustered, he felt some of his old shyness return and grasped for things to say. Lynda smiled and nodded without looking at him.

"Yes, it sure is." She seemed much more self-assured than he felt. But her voice, softer than it had been earlier, carried a strain of vulnerability. As she drained the last of her water, she leaned down, planting her empty water bottle in the sand, and tried to act nonchalant.

As he surveyed the scene, he couldn't help but notice the irony of his situation. He was watching fireworks and feeling fireworks. Something like static electricity tingled all over his body and he felt positively giddy. He couldn't remember how long it had been since he felt this crushy energy.

And for the past two years, Myrna had been too sick for affection or intimacy. She was so fragile the last few months that he couldn't even hug her. At the time, he thought nothing of it. His focus was centered on her care from day to day. But now, an exhilarating hunger for what he'd missed without knowing it, and the luxurious sensation of its sudden return, overwhelmed him.

He felt utterly startled at this delightful possibility being dangled in front of him like manna from Heaven. This was a ride and he wasn't asking any questions. With the conviction of a man so recently touched and irrevocably changed by death, he knew in his bones that life was too short for that. And in this moment, he was grateful for the knowledge, which was in itself another wondrous step in the direction of life. This was a chance he didn't know if he'd ever get again, however much he might've longed for it. Now, his usual refrain *new and different* reverberated in his mind, taking on entirely new connotations.

They sat in silence until the fireworks became more and more sporadic, the moon rose higher, and people began trickling away. As friends gathered their belongings, they came over to say their goodbyes. Mel stood, releasing Lynda's hand, and hugged their friends warmly. As Lynda rose, Brandy and Billy ran up to say they were riding home with the Savellis. It was time to go, and Lynda was keenly aware that Mel was leaving again tomorrow to fly back to his motorhome out west. What did it all mean? Was he feeling the same?

When it was time for them to trickle away, he folded up Lynda's chair, slipped it over his shoulder, reached out with his hand and, gently and wordlessly, took hers.

What the hell was that, Lynda thought as she groaned and clasped the steering wheel of her car. Most of the other cars had pulled away, imbuing the parking lot with a wilted, abandoned feeling. She laid her forehead against the steering wheel and forced herself to exhale fully and calmly. Mel had just walked her to her car, wished her goodnight, and, after she situated herself in the driver's seat, shut the car door behind her. Now, she waited for Gerry to return from the restroom, giving Lynda a few moments of precious alone time.

She tilted her head up from the steering wheel and peeked at the digital clock glaring from the dashboard. 10:45. Pangs of exhaustion coursed under a light-headed wakefulness. She felt buzzed even though she only drank a couple beers much earlier in the evening. But this wasn't a buzz. It was a crush. A crazy, inexplicable crush on one of her best friends blooming in the midst of confusion. A strong sense of doubt wrecked her responses. She wanted to skip down the street, go to sleep, and groan – all at the same time.

Her mind returned to the scene of Mel's goodbye. He hadn't said 'goodnight' exactly. What he'd said was "Keep in touch." That was right after he folded her in the cozy blanket of his embrace. It was a completely normal thing for him to say to her, a maddeningly typical hug. But something about the way he held her hand as they walked off the beach felt charged, more solid. Friends didn't really do that – even in RYL. That was a boyfriend thing. That was the real sign that he felt something.

She lifted her head and saw Gerry walking towards the car. Gerry opened the car door, plopped down, exhilarated by the evening. She began chatting as Lynda reversed the car. Even though Lynda tried to focus, she felt floaty and couldn't stop trying to process the evening. But Gerry, aflutter with her grandson's new romance, didn't seem to notice.

"Did you notice how Nick stayed by Brandy's side all night?" Gerry asked. The air was relatively cool and Lynda cracked her window, sliding her hand out to ride the wind as they drove. "And what about those fireworks – I couldn't believe some of them. Can you imagine how much they cost?" Frankly, Lynda thought, that was easier to imagine than what happened to her tonight. "And it was so wonderful to have Mel back in town – he seems to be doing so well."

Lynda agreed, keeping her eyes nailed to the road. Gerry's chatter reminded Lynda of an all-you-can-eat buffet, a little something here, a little something there. Lynda could just pop in and out of the conversation as she wanted without much fuss. It was unusual for Gerry to be so talkative, but Lynda was grateful because it meant she didn't have to speak. She'd never been very good at hiding her feelings and didn't really understand why people tried so hard to do that anyway. Still, she didn't want to say anything until she felt clearer about what, if anything, had happened between her and Mel. And, for some reason, she was also anxious about how Gerry might respond.

"Lynda, you okay? You seem unusually quiet." Lynda stared past Gerry, then looked at her, the truth percolating up as soon as she made eye contact. She had to say something, the only thing she could be certain of. She wasn't even sure what it would be until it came out of her mouth. She paused and took a breath. She couldn't believe the words that were getting ready to leave her mouth.

"Gerry, I think I'm attracted to Mel!"

CHAPTER TWENTY-FOUR
KEEP IN TOUCH

For a torturous moment, they were both silent. Lynda couldn't help worrying about what Gerry might think – what with Mel recently widowed. And he was one of the leaders of their community. Even though he was one of her best friends, he was also a mentor and teacher. Something about him still felt distant, untouchable, because she looked up to him. What did it all mean? And what, if she figured that out, would everyone else think about it? His wife just died four months ago, for God's sake. Was he even ready to date? And, this next question approached seamlessly, with stealth. Was she really good enough to be his partner?

For too many years of her life, she would've naively accepted this question.

Now, after so many incarnations and variations of it, she recognized it for what it was, a toxic remnant of unworthiness submerged beneath her scars. She'd let insecurity cripple her for so long, even in her relationship with Wade. But now, she had an opportunity to love herself the way she deserved. She breathed and refocused her thoughts, at last settling on another question. Would a romance with Mel ruin their friendship, a friendship she treasured?

It was at this moment that Gerry looked at her evenly and finally broke her silence. "Well, I think that's just perfect," she exclaimed, excitement in her voice. Lynda, who'd been leaning tensely towards Gerry, relaxed back into her seat, a little stunned. She felt incredulous.

"You do?"

"Well, yes!" Gerry answered, as if it were the most obvious thing in the world. Then she drew a package of chewing gum out of her purse, took out a piece out, and offered it wordlessly to Lynda. Then she unwrapped another and popped it playfully in her mouth. Gerry was normally so sedate that Lynda wondered if the evening's new romances were bringing out a bit of her inner child. She looked into Lynda's eyes. "Listen, I've been around a long time and these wrinkles mean more than old age. I know a thing or two about men." Her eyes fogged up slightly, then unclouded. "When I lost my Frank, I knew I'd never find anyone else, didn't want to or need to. But most men . . . they need someone to, you know, take care of them. And Mel takes care of so many people. All of us really." She paused, then shrugged. "Who's taking care of him?"

"Well, I guess I never thought about it like that," Lynda admitted.

"And he needs someone in the community, someone who knows RYL. That's his life, his whole way of being in the world. And . . . now that I think about it, I can't think of anyone I'd rather put him with than you."

"Really?" Lynda's relief was palpable, her anxiety easing. Maybe she wasn't so crazy after all.

"Really," Gerry answered, right before she blew a big, pink bubble like a teenager. Then she added, for play or emphasis or both, "Really, really." Lynda, more grateful for this wonder named Gerry than she'd ever been, joined her friend in a rich, throaty laugh.

Back at Cindy's place, Mel let the cat slip through the door as it whispered shut behind him. It was late and, except for his room, the carpeted house was hushed and dark. He always stayed with Cindy when he was in town and, because he'd always liked cats, appreciated the opportunity to spend time with her cat. It made it feel a little more like home. He placed his wallet on the dresser and tossed his faded, leather planner in the chair that sat beside the dresser. For a moment, he regarded the planner, which had faithfully held his notes, jottings, pictures and calendars for many years. It was where he'd tucked his Ideal Partner list. And now, it held his flight itinerary back to Colorado and the Loft. He was leaving in the morning and wouldn't return to Florida for a month, until it was time to teach the next course.

He tucked his t-shirt and shorts into an already-packed suitcase which lay open on the desk. His clothes for the flight were arranged on top. His business papers were already packed into the black canvas messenger bag he took everywhere. He got into bed, stretched his legs in front of him, and folded his hands on his lap. Pictures from the evening paraded one after another in his mind. The high that had enveloped him earlier faded as he looked around Cindy's guest room. All seemed back to normal, yet different. He thought about saying good night to Lynda. He felt he'd successfully warded off his feelings of awkwardness, and most everything had felt so easy, like a sheet of music he read effortlessly. Until he said goodbye and he hadn't known what to say.

As he stood with her at her car, something had changed, but deciding exactly what it was and acknowledging it to her proved more difficult, if it was even appropriate. When the time came, he let go of her hand, embraced her, looked into her eyes and fell to habit, saying "keep in touch." That's what he would've said before tonight – what he would've said when they were just friends. Everyone thought he was such an extrovert, but he'd always struggled with shyness. Maybe it had been that, or maybe he was just really out of his comfort zone.

Now, as he recalled his words, they hung pregnant with both unspoken meaning and inadequacy. Pangs of doubt and anxiety deflated his former giddiness. The fact was that Lynda never confirmed whether she felt a connection, and he hadn't asked. How could he be sure she shared his interpretation of what happened tonight? He ran his fingers through his hair, still lustrous and thick, and sighed audibly.

Just then the cat, a lush, long-haired brindle, jumped on the bed beside him and began padding his leg with its paws. Her fur ran silky under his palm as he stroked her. An unbidden image of Lynda sitting under the moonlight rushed back to him, injecting him with a curious combination of happiness, shock, and adrenaline. The image of her beautiful profile as she gazed towards the dark ocean seemed etched in his brain. In his picture of her, her features warmed under the fireworks, then glowed cool under the moon. Lynda, formerly one of his closest friends, had revealed the face of an enticing stranger to him. He placed the cat on the floor, and reaching towards the bedside table to turn off the light, decided against it.

Despite his early flight in the morning, he knew it would be some time before he got any rest.

CHAPTER TWENTY-FIVE
TEN THOUSAND LESSONS

At five minutes past eight the following Friday morning, Lynda entered the hushed, air-conditioned waiting room of the Physician's Group offices. She'd spent the last few days contemplating what had happened with Mel and what it meant. Which is to say she spent a lot of time stewing in uncertainty and doubt, which was her habit. Because of this, she still hadn't told anyone yet except Gerry. This morning she was nearly bursting with desire to tell someone else and get some more feedback. As she traversed the small waiting area lined with chairs, potted plants and side tables presenting tidy stacks of magazines, she knew just who to talk to.

Liz, the office's administrator extraordinaire, sat behind the reception counter, her head bobbing to the pop music she liked to play on the "down low," as she called it. Liz, who had a heart the size of Texas and a mouth to match, was a single mom with a ten-year-old son. And her ex wasn't the gentle type, which explained why Liz was so quick to commiserate with Lynda over Wade's "gas-lighting," another of Liz's phrases. She tapped the counter with her knuckle to get Liz's attention.

"Oh, hey girl," Liz said as she slid the window out of the way, beaming a bright smile. "I was just gettin' ready to turn on the tunes and open the office." Liz loved hip-hop, but since most of it was too edgy for the office, she played thumpy dance pop instead. Lynda could see that Liz had already started chipping away at the day's paperwork as she stood up, swiveled to the side, and popped a form into a wall file labeled "Insurance Follow-Up." Physician's Group provided wellness treatments to car accident victims, so Liz handled a mountain of insurance paperwork. Lynda worked as the Licensed Massage Therapist on staff. The job wasn't glamorous, but it was Lynda's first job out of massage therapy school. And she liked the fact that it provided an opportunity to learn. Besides giving massages, she learned how to administer electric stimulation, traction, and ultrasound. She loved her work helping people, especially when she was able to share a bit of knowledge to improve a patient's health. Between Physician's Group and teaching fitness classes part-time at the Y, she supported herself and her children just fine.

"How are you today, Miss Liz?" Liz shrugged and chuckled.

"Oh, you know. Same stuff, different morning."

"We've been so busy I haven't had a chance to ask you what you did for the fourth. How did it go?"

"Oh, you know. Same stuff, different year, I suppose. My son went to a friend's house, and I just hung out at my house. How 'bout you?" Lynda's eyes lit up. She leaned in towards Liz, now standing opposite of her on the other side of the counter.

"I had a fantastic time." Liz, sensing a juicy conversation, raised a conspicuous eyebrow and put her hand on her hip.

"Well, you're not just going to stand there are you? Let's get some coffee and chat. I'll come 'round and let you in." Liz left the reception area, unlocked the door that allowed patients into the treatment area of the office, and pulled the door open for Lynda.

Lynda followed Liz into the break room, where she flipped the lights on, hoisted her bag on a table, and started the coffee. Liz sat down and rapped her fingers, one after another, on the tabletop. The sound of her long, painted nails clicked in the empty room behind Lynda.

"Spill them beans, now, and tell me what got you in such a state," Liz said.

"Well," Lynda started as she finished pouring coffee grains into the coffee machine and closed its lid. "I told you how I was going out with my RYL friends, right?"

"You mean the cult?" Liz was jokingly referring to RYL.

"Yeah, that one," Lynda joked before becoming serious once more. She turned the tap on and held the coffee pot beneath it. "We all went out to dinner and then to Indian Shores beach. I was sitting on the beach with my friends Mel and Deb and," Lynda trailed off before adding cautiously, "we made a connection. At least . . . I think we did."

At this an expression of ironic amusement laced Liz's face. "Wait – you and Deb made a connection? Or you and Mel made a connection?" Lynda giggled. Leave it to Liz.

"Me and Mel."

"He's the leader? Of the cult, I mean?" Lynda rolled her eyes.

"He's the one who teaches the workshops," she said, joining Liz at the table. "Along with some others."

"Well, at least he's got his crap together. I mean, you've gotta have your crap together to successfully lead a cult." Lynda laughed at Liz's joke even though she couldn't help feeling a tad offended. She wished Liz would back off the cult jokes. Lynda had shared RYL with Liz in the past. But even though Liz listened intently and agreed that changing your life was a good idea, there was always some reason she couldn't enroll in the workshop. Lynda suspected her jokes were a not-so-subtle defense against change. Over the years, Lynda had seen this response more times than she could count, and she empathized and related to it. There had been a time in her life when she was resistant to changing her life because it meant seeing things she didn't want to see, confronting things she didn't want to confront. It was downright challenging, but the rewards were extraordinary. And she'd always been the kind of person who sought out opportunities to recover what was lost, to improve life for its own sake, and to live regret-free.

"He does," Lynda agreed, adding, "He's the one who lost his wife recently." At this, Liz grew more somber. Even she had scruples about poking fun at a recent widower. Lynda continued. "We were just sitting there holding hands like we always do but then . . . well, I guess I started to rub his hand like a girlfriend would. At least, that's what it felt like. I didn't even realize I was doing it at first."

Liz shifted in her seat as the aroma of fresh-brewed coffee filled the air. "So you made the first move?"

"It wasn't a move exactly. And I didn't know I was doing it. When I realized it, I stopped. But then . . ."

Liz looked at her expectantly. "But then . . ."

"Then *he* started rubbing *my* hand. And it felt like there was a real connection." The coffeepot sputtered and went silent. "I mean, there was a real connection, at least for me," she added, frowning a little.

It was crystal clear to Liz that Lynda was experiencing a lot of doubt. She rallied to encourage her friend. "Well, that's wonderful, Lynda. What's not wonderful about that?"

"I guess I'm just a little concerned about his age. I think he's like twenty years older than me. And . . . there's our friendship. I'm afraid dating him might damage it."

Liz considered this as she got up, pulled two coffee cups from a cupboard, and began to fill them. She looked back at Lynda. "You like a little sugar, right?" she asked, her bluesy voice resonant with a melodic flourish.

"Just a little," Lynda replied. Liz grabbed a small packet of sugar and handed it, along with a hot cup of coffee, to Lynda. Then she sat down, cradling her cup in her hands, and eyed Lynda.

"After everything I've seen you go through with Wade, I think you need someone who's mature, who's got his act together. And Wade ain't never gonna' be that." Lynda sipped her coffee. A pang of sadness and frustration moved through her.

"I know you're right about Wade. I can't even get him to sign off on the divorce papers. It's like pulling teeth."

"Divorce papers! I thought you called off the wedding – you ain't even married yet!" Liz was incredulous.

"Oh, yeah," Lynda said sheepishly. She realized she hadn't shared about her and Wade being legally married. "We actually got married a few months ago in secret. Our big wedding ceremony that I called off would've been for our friends and families." Liz clicked her tongue and shook her head the way she often did when she was right about something, which she often was.

"He don't want to lose you Lynda. He's still hoping you'll come back and take care of him 'cause that baby-man can't take care of himself."

"Tell me about it. I'm paying for the divorce and he's still living in my rental house, for God's sake." As she said this, she recalled another bitter complication of the split. "He also owes me money. I'll probably never see that again."

"I even gave him back my ring, after everything he owes me."

"I guess you payed to learn a good lesson," Liz said. Lynda sighed, a hint of resigned anger in her voice. "I've asked and asked, but I just have no idea how to get that man to sign the papers. I don't want the ring. I just want to be done." At this, both women were quiet for a moment, lost perhaps, in silent exasperation over all the empty promises they'd both heard over the years.

Lynda tried not to feel bitter as she peered into her cup. "That's a lot of damn lessons," she muttered. Liz looked at her in empathy.

"Does it matter, babe? All that matters is that you finally learned. You finally learned." Lynda stared at her friend in astonishment. Maybe Liz didn't need RYL so much after all.

CHAPTER TWENTY-SIX
PROCRASTINATION

Shortly before quitting time, Lynda bid her last client of the week goodbye, pulled the dirty sheets from her massage table, and flipped the overhead light on. She made sure to include little spa touches like dim lighting even though, technically, this was a clinical setting. She didn't have to use salt lamps or candles, but she knew it helped her clients relax, and this made her work much more effective. Yes, she had to buy these extra touches on her own dime, but she didn't mind. She bent down and blew a candle out, inhaling its sweet, juicy scent as its smoke permeated the room. Besides, she thought as she reared up and looked around her treatment room with satisfaction, she liked all the extras, too.

Of course, like any job worth doing, massage therapy had its challenges. Her clients came to her for relief from injury, so she heard her fair share of complaining. She often found it challenging to get them to pipe down and relax as she massaged them. It didn't take her long to learn after starting the job that it was best to take the direct route and counsel them before their first massage. She started with a brief overview of their nervous system and how it related to relaxation and physical healing.

Then she counseled them with pithy "tips," one of which was her "breathing instead of talking" tip. Even her chattiest clients would quiet down after about five minutes. This was often the moment when she could actually feel their muscles begin to melt under her hands, when her real work began.

Lynda sat down at the small work counter and regarded a short pile of files. She picked up a file, opened it, and began to write. Today she had five clients, so each of their files needed notes. She didn't have a dedicated office, so she had to complete paperwork in the treatment room or the break room. On days like today, when she wanted to clear out of the office quickly, she completed her paperwork undisturbed in the treatment room. After that it was just a matter of tidying up, restocking, grabbing her bag, and dropping the files off with Liz on her way out, a routine that usually lasted no more than twenty minutes. This might have been when the two women would mention having dinner together, as they often did, but it never happened. This was probably a good thing, because tonight all she wanted to do was get home and call Wade. If she had to hound him for the divorce papers, then so be it.

She was tired of procrastinating. She was even more tired of feeling apprehensive. It was better to just get the ordeal over with. She'd spent three years feeling afraid and walking on eggshells around him. She was done wasting time. Even though she still wasn't sure what she was going to say or how she was going to end their deadlock, she was committed to calling him right after dinner in the hopes he'd sign the papers in time to file them on Monday.

Thirty minutes later she drove down Renellie Drive, a wide, tree-lined street she'd called home for years. Even though her house was within walking distance of work, she drove to avoid walking in the heat in her scrubs. She and her first husband had bought the house on Renellie the year Brandy was born. It was a modest, single-level, three-bedroom – a home her mom once called the "perfect starter house" when she was in one of her better moods. Similar homes with large, geometric yards in various states of grooming lined the street on both sides. They had so much fun renovating the home the month before moving in, adding new paint, carpeting, and fixtures while Brandy, just a baby, played on a blanket.

Lynda noticed the front door hanging wide open as she pulled into the driveway. For some reason, her teenagers couldn't remember to close doors behind them, something she was forever reminding them to do. She even threatened them with paying the electric bill one month. She walked in, kicked her shoes off, set her bag down, and headed towards the kitchen for some water. As she cut through the dining room, she saw Billy hunched over a bowl at the dining table spooning cereal into his mouth. Tall and lanky with chestnut hair, he generally only came out of his bedroom when he was hungry. Tonight, he looked a little moody but, like most fifteen-year olds, he looked like that a lot. She'd gotten used to it. He seemed happier since attending the RYL weekend, and she hoped and prayed that he'd continue to figure things out. She kissed him on top of the head, ruffling his curls as she passed.

"Hey, Mom," he mumbled. Lynda could see and hear him as she puttered around the kitchen because it opened onto the dining room.

"Hey! Eating all the Rice Krispies again, I see," Lynda teased. He shrugged.

"Just woke up from a nap."

"I thought you'd be at work still?" Billy had just increased his hours at work, since she and his dad had agreed to let him drop out of school and get his GED. Lynda didn't want to, but his GPA was already so low that he wouldn't graduate anyway. She accepted that she wasn't a perfect parent, but sometimes, she couldn't help but agonize over any choices she'd made that might have caused the situation. Like Wade, Billy's father considered military school, but Lynda thought it was better to encourage a sense of responsibility through working, and Billy agreed. Billy upended the bowl and drank the pinkish, cereal-flavored milk.

"Got off early," he said.

Then she heard Brandy call from her bedroom, "Mom, is that you?"

"In the kitchen, Sweetie!" Lynda called back. She heard Brandy's bedroom door opening moments before she whisked into the kitchen, opened the refrigerator, and squinted into it. Her wavy, golden hair was a little more reddish than Billy's, but neither of them got Lynda's ginger-red hair. Brandy wore a peach t-shirt with a gold sun and rainbow on it. It was a lot like her personality, Lynda thought with affection. People had always told Lynda that parenting a teenage daughter would be tough, but Brandy was easy.

Billy had turned out to be the challenging one.

"We need some food," Brandy whined, still gazing into the fridge.

"Well," Lynda said, taking a sip of ice water, "feel like going to the store with me tonight?" Brandy sighed dramatically and shut the refrigerator door.

"Why not?" she said to her mom. Brandy was the oldest, and for the most part, she was generally mature and responsible. But she was still a teenager. She'd never expected to have to parent two teenagers by herself, but they had created a happy life. And she felt that, all in all, her kids were relatively easy. Just then Billy entered the kitchen and placed his bowl in the sink.

"I'm gonna' wash this later," he said to no one in particular.

"Sure." Lynda said to him. "Like you're going to close the front door every day."

Billy smirked at Brandy, saying, "That was Brandy."

"Was not!" Brandy bantered back. Then she paused, her voice tinged with guilt. "Okay, maybe it was."

"Yeah, Brandy," Billy teased. "You're an adult now, aren't you? Shouldn't you be able to remember things like that in your old age?" At this Brandy made a little crying sound, exaggerating her voice to a slow whine.

"Mom," she said, stretching the word out and shaking her head, "make him stop."

Instead, Lynda decided to join in. "Brandy you *are* going to be nineteen in November, right?"

Brandy collapsed on the countertop. "You people are being hard on me! I just forgot today, okay? But you know me – I'm normally so good about that." Lynda smiled warmly at her kids. They almost made her forget the unpleasantness of calling Wade.

"That's okay," she said, "We'll just dock a dollar off of your birthday money for every time you leave the front door open." Billy laughed, regarding his mom with a mischievous gleam.

"That means I get the extra, right? My birthday is in November, too." Before Lynda could answer, she heard her cell phone ringing and walked to the living room to answer it. She steeled herself as she looked at the screen to see who was calling. Maybe it would be Wade.

It was her mom.

CHAPTER TWENTY-SEVEN
COACHING

"I haven't talked to you in ages!" her mother gushed. Then she asked with a sympathetic tone, "How's the divorce going, Sweetie?" Lynda listened carefully to her mom's voice, trying to read her mood, hesitating for a moment before responding.

"Good," Lynda answered cheerfully. Then she added, "but slow."

"Oh," her mother said, though in a tone that really meant *of course*. And that little phrase *of course* could go in a number of directions because her mother excelled at irony and double speak, features of her unique quicksand conversational style, a style that could pull Lynda in before she knew it. Then again, today her mom sounded good. Pleasant even.

"Well, Honey," her mom continued as if she was chatting breezily with friends at the golf club, "Wade was never good for you. We all knew that."

Lynda frowned as she sat on the couch. She tried to determine who her mom might be referring to. "You did? Who knew that?"

"Your brothers, honey," her mom answered, as if it were completely obvious. "I mean, I was on the phone with Joe just last night, and he told me that he was so glad Wade was finally out of your life." Sometimes her mom sounded exactly like a televangelist. Lynda felt a familiar sense of unease. While she knew it was naive to believe that family members never talked about one another, knowing it always made her feel naked and vulnerable, especially when it came to her mother.

Her mom was a powerful, complex woman of many moods and strong opinions, someone Lynda and her brothers had learned to sidestep and placate as a matter of course. And her mom's alcoholism didn't help matters. Lynda had spent years attempting to understand how the alcohol and pills might've warped her mom's behavior over time. But a large part of her still viewed her mother as unforgivable for the way she'd treated her. Her mom also had her loving moments, but they were hard to discern through the haze of resentment and toxicity Lynda felt.

Lynda picked at her scrubs, grown nubby with wear. She tried and failed to tell if her mom had been drinking tonight or not. She thought her brothers liked Wade.

"Perhaps he mentioned something like that once." Lynda said simply.

Her mom cooed in a show of support. "I just hate to see you go through this, Honey." Even though her mom's words made her feel suspicious, they also comforted her. Her mom sounded almost protective, and despite everything, Lynda could hear that deep down, her mom loved her. Lynda couldn't remember a time when her mother had been stable or felt safe. And she knew this is why she'd learned to be hyper-vigilant, especially with her mom. It was a common trait among adult children of alcoholics. But it was also confusing and exhausting. Sometimes, she couldn't distinguish between her own projections and her mom's actual behavior.

Lynda heard raised voices from the kitchen area. "You all quiet down, okay!" she yelled to Brandy and Billy, still goofing around in the kitchen. "I'm on the phone!" Then, in a hopeful tone to her mom: "You know I'm feeling really good, Mom.

Like, better than I have in years, like I'm shedding skin or something." Then she paused and added, "I'm just not sad."

"You know, Lynda," her mom replied, almost giddy, "that is *exactly* how I felt when I divorced your dad." A bolt of confusion shot through Lynda. *Her dad?* she thought incredulously. For a long time, she hadn't understood how much he'd done to save his marriage. Her mom was the one who was addicted to who-knows-what and having all kinds of affairs. Lynda knew good people did bad things, and so wanted all of it to stay in the past. But comments like this, even if they were caused by something Lynda barely understood, drew blood. Her mom just couldn't seem to let it rest.

Lynda would never forget the day she watched her dad walk down the stairs with his suitcase in hand. As a child, she was devastated, terrified, at the thought of her dad leaving. His decision not to leave seemed like a miracle. But later, after Lynda became an adult, she realized that he had decided not to leave for her and her brothers. He endured and sacrificed one more year . . . for them.

For her.

She forced herself to remain quiet as her mom continued. "I mean, he was terrible to me, just no good." Lynda's adrenaline surged. This wasn't the first time her mom had blamed her dad for their divorce. *He was terrible to her? How could she compare Wade to my father?* Her dad was one of the most selfless men she knew. He couldn't live with her mom, but he'd always done everything he possibly could for her. Lynda was furious.

"They're not the same at all, Mom," she snapped. "Wade is nothing – and I mean *nothing* – like Dad. "I don't understand how –"

"There's a lot you don't know, Lynda," her mom interrupted. "He left me all by myself all the time. And . . . he was terrible in bed, you know." Lynda gasped. Even though her mom often said outrageous things, Lynda couldn't help but feel utter shock every single time. She never got used to it. What's more, she was angry at herself for letting her guard down. Her knuckles turned white. She felt her anger boiling out of control like it often did in times of stress.

"I've got to go now," Lynda replied. It was the only thing she could get out without screaming.

"Lynda, what is wrong with you —" her mom said in an accusatory tone.

"I've just got to go. I'll talk to you later." Lynda ended the call as quickly as possible, wishing she had the luxury of a corded phone so she could slam a receiver into a cradle. She narrowed her eyes. This conversation was only headed to a bad place, and she didn't need that right now. She just didn't have time for her mother's . . . whatever it was. She knew that some kind of mental illness likely caused her mom's bizarre behavior, but she was still left with the reality of trying to cope, and it always left her feeling miserable. And completely inadequate. What was she supposed to do? To think, to feel?

All her life, her mother got the award for being her codependence coach. And when she let herself get hooked back into it, shame and confusion returned like ugly, old ghosts.

She had no more words, not for her mom and not for Wade.

She put her head in her hands, deflated at the thought of calling Wade. The conversation with her mom had drained her. There was no way she had the energy to confront Wade tonight.

The next day, Lynda steered her bike east towards Ballast Point Park. The mid-afternoon sun, low and assisted by light gusts of wind, felt like a soothing caress. Because the Point jutted out into a corner of Hillsborough Bay, it was often cool and breezy, a feature that made it popular with locals. Its biggest draw was a well-appointed, four-hundred-foot pier from which the entire skyline of downtown Tampa unfolded on the horizon, the waters studded with brilliant sunbeams.

The ride passed quickly, and she found herself curving up the park's bike path before she knew it. She slowed down, taking in the mangroves and blue water edging the path. She was so close that if she fell off the bike on the wrong side, she might land right in the water – a fearsome thought since it was peppered with rocks. These same rocks made perfect perches for birds, however, and Lynda spotted a large, white crane only a few yards out. A smattering of people meandered around, engaged in various activities and conversations. More than a few attended fishing lines on a smaller pier that paralleled the big one. As she hopped off her bike, she waved to a couple snacking at a table on a cafe patio. It nestled at the entrance of the big pier facing the water and doubled as a bait and tackle shop.

As she walked up the pier and soaked in the view, she became aware of her cell phone jostling awkwardly in her pocket. She reached in her pocket and grabbed it, balancing it with her handlebar as she walked. It had been four days since the fireworks, and Mel had said "Keep in touch." She wanted to reach out, but the thought of calling him unnerved her.

How would she be received? Would she be the friend she'd always been, or something more?

Maybe she'd discover that there had been no actual connection – that it was all in her imagination. She needed to know.

The situation with Wade still weighed on her mind. She knew she needed to brave a conversation with him, but she still struggled with what to say. But Mel could help her find a solution. He was the voice of reason, and she respected his advice.

She pulled her bike to the side and leaned against the railing, taking in the serene view of Tampa Bay. The gentle rippling of the waves had a calming effect on her nerves. She pulled out her cell phone, took a deep breath, and dialed Mel's number.

She felt anxious. For the briefest moment, a tiny part of her hoped she'd get his voice mail. The idea of leaving a message just felt a little less vulnerable. She chewed her lip as she wondered if she should play it cool or ask him about July fourth. Before she had a chance to decide, she heard his voice, clear and upbeat as ever.

"Hello, Lynda? Is that you?"

CHAPTER TWENTY-EIGHT
SUNSHINE

Mel suppressed a disorienting sense of school-boy eagerness when he saw Lynda's name pop up on his phone. He was visiting Mark in Colorado again. He covered the phone's receiver with his hand, asking over his shoulder in a calm, hushed voice, "Mark, will you turn down the music a bit?"

Mark quickly dialed down the volume as Mel turned back to the phone and said, "Hello . . ."

"Hey Mel, I was just thinking about you." Lynda's familiar voice felt like an embrace, amplifying the strange satisfaction that began when he saw her name. He and Mark had just been talking about going to their favorite restaurant for ribs when her call instigated his retreat from Mark's cleverly designed living room. Now he stood in the quiet sanctuary of the foyer. A blow-up mattress he used when he stayed the night sat propped against the wall. He felt the bashfulness creeping up again and tried not to let it seep into his voice.

"It's great to hear from you. How are things back in Florida?"

Lynda gazed out over the bay and cleared her throat a little. The small talk soothed her nerves. She hoped he didn't realize what she'd been thinking about right before she called, but at the same time, she wished he would. "Oh, good," she said. "I just rode my bike to Ballast Point, and I'm sitting on the pier enjoying the sunshine."

Mel glanced at his watch. It was only four-thirty in Denver. "We're gearing up for a little dinner," he said, "but I have no ocean to enjoy, so I'll have to make do with the Rockies."

"Glad you made it back safely, by the way," she said, donning a quiet, bemused smile. She furrowed her brow a little, trying to remember why, exactly, she'd called him. Then it came to her. Wade. "So I wanted to ask your advice about Wade," she said, shifting into their habitual dynamic of close friends.

"Shoot. I'm listening."

"I've been calling Wade, but he still doesn't seem willing to sign the papers. Half the time, he doesn't even respond to my calls, and I'm not sure why. I feel like it's because . . ." She had a peculiar habit of letting her thoughts evaporate as she spoke.

As he listened, Mel nodded his head slightly. This was Wade's M.O., he thought, but there had to be a way to get him moving. "It's a way to keep you under control, Lynda." Then he added, "When someone refuses to play, they hijack the game."

"That's what I thought, too. It's a power thing."

"Maybe, but he also probably doesn't want to let go of you, either." Lynda agreed.

"I need to figure out what to say so he knows that it's over, and he'll just sign off." Her voice was adamant.

Mel considered. He'd always found that being forthright was the best route in situations like this. "Be direct," he said simply. "He's already got the papers, right?"

"Yes, they've been at his house for a couple of weeks."

"Then call him up tonight or tomorrow, tell him they need to be signed by a particular day, and you'll stop by after work to pick them up." Lynda tucked her hair behind her ear. He made it sound so simple. Then she paused.

Maybe it really was that simple.

"I can do that," she said, invigorated. The energy in her voice reminded Mel of why he'd always enjoyed her friendship so much. Then, he felt an abnormal swell of enthusiasm as he leaned against the wall. He pictured her sitting on the pier, her hair glinting copper in the sun. He remembered how soft her skin felt when he held her hand and wished he could hold it again. The longing to be near her sharpened. He wondered if he should mention anything about July fourth. Then he heard her chuckle.

"Who knows?" she said. "Maybe this will all be over with by the time you come back for the next course."

"Maybe you'll even have it done by next week," he encouraged. If there was one person who deserved the best, he thought, it was Lynda. She'd been with RYL since the inaugural season six years before, and while he'd seen her struggle, he'd also witnessed considerable growth in her self-esteem and personal power. As a teacher, it was gratifying to have a student like her that worked so hard to overcome her own patterns. Not all of his students were as conscientious.

Lynda was unable to detect any spark lurking behind the small talk and friendly advice, but she still wasn't certain. Sometimes, he seemed to play his cards close to his chest, and she found him hard to read. It was too hard to discern over the phone. Still trying to feel him out, she made a bold decision. In her side-vision, she noted a fish vaulting from the water as she steadied her nerves.

"You'll come home before the next course in August, right?" she asked nonchalantly.

"I've already bought my ticket. I'll arrive on Wednesday."

Lynda held her breath and hesitated. Then she took the plunge. "I was wondering if you'd like to come to dinner with me and the kids on Thursday while you're in town?"

Mel was delighted. Scenes from the night of the fourth had replayed in his mind over the past three days, and he enjoyed the feelings it stirred within him. For a man who was methodical and typically analyzed a given situation, it was unusual for him to be so completely immersed in emotion. But there was nothing normal or familiar about his life these days. It was "new and different," and thoughts of Lynda lit up his spirit, and he felt delightfully happy. He didn't stop to question what it all meant or if she felt the same way, he simply relished in his excitement.

Oh my goodness! He felt like the high school cheerleader had just asked him to the prom. "Sure," he replied. "I'd like that."

Though she could feel her relief and excitement overflowing, Lynda prayed it didn't come across over the phone. "Great! We can have dinner on Thursday –"

Not being able to help himself, Mel interjected. "It's the 3rd ... August the 3rd."

Lynda smiled again. She loved Mel's plain-spoken style. His words always sounded definitive, clean feeling somehow. Strong, crisp, and truthful. Right now, they filled her with inexplicable delight. "Okay, August the 3rd it is then," she said as they said good-bye.

CHAPTER TWENTY-NINE
WAITING

Later that night, Mel sat hunched on his bed in the Loft, staring down at something intently. He'd driven to Mark's and found a space in an RV park in Golden Colorado. Soon he'd fly to Melanie's to celebrate Joshie's first birthday. Ever since Myrna died, he felt a special connection to Myrna whenever he was with Joshie. Maybe it was attending Joshie's birth that had inspired him and Myrna to move into the Loft in the first place. Or, that holding Joshie had been her dying wish, a wish granted as she took her last breath.

He didn't know.

He stared down at a stack of glossy photographs he held in his hands. An open drawer nearly touched his knees as he sorted through them. The last time he'd looked at them was back in June, after developing them in New Orleans. He'd tucked them away and forgotten about them until tonight. Now he remembered.

Image after image of the ravaged Ninth Ward scrolled before him. Miasmic scrap yards that were once neighborhoods. Fluorescent orange X's spray-painted on faded sidings, numbers counting survivors and deceased in its four quadrants. The last photo was a single picture of Myrna that he'd taken back in February, a month before she died.

She'd walked out of the Loft's tiny bedroom one evening, sat on her favorite sofa and said – no, demanded – "Take my picture." She'd sounded resolute yet resigned, as if the request took all her energy. Knowing she didn't like to have her picture taken Mel had questioned why. But Myrna was unwavering. "Just take my picture." *Yes, dear.*

He didn't know it then, but it would be her last photograph. Now, sitting here, he could barely bring himself to look at it.

In the picture, she gazed up at him through sunken hollows, the smoky brown of her eyes consumed in shadow. Her face pinched, a gaunt, sallow shade of what it once was. Her petite frame, made slighter and more brittle by months of cancer, at rest beneath her gray sweatshirt.

He shook his head, tucked the pictures back into their envelope, and shut them in the drawer. Then he paused, his hand still clasped on the handle. All the events and threads of the last year seemed to convene here, in this moment, jostling for space. Myrna, the Loft, Joshie's first birthday, his travels. Lynda.

It all felt surreal.

He could also feel faint tendrils of grief, once so familiar, begin to creep through his body.

He noticed his glass of wine sitting untouched on a side table beside the bed. It seemed random and strange, like a prop some stagehand forgot to remove. Teeming with memories, he closed his eyes. The Loft seemed to breathe around him as the full realization that today was an anniversary of sorts overcame him.

Marked by Joshie's birth, it was nearly the Loft's one-year anniversary.

When Myrna and Mel had packed up their RV to go to Minnesota, it hadn't been the Loft, but an older used RV they'd purchased for the trip. After the month with Melanie and family in Minnesota, they motored to North Dakota for an RV rally. Myrna felt relatively strong then, but the pain management was a constant balancing act with her medication. Too little and she still suffered, too much and it knocked her out. They hoped for a cure and prayed for a miracle.

They hardly ever referred to it – the cancer. But when they did, positive affirmations were the language they used. He remembered feeling surprised when Myrna looked at him that weekend and said, "I'd like to drive out of here in a new RV." They wasted no time picking out "the Loft." It was a 34-foot National Dolphin, and they settled in before driving to Montreal to visit Myrna's family.

It felt like a new beginning, not their last home together.

Mel opened his eyes and glimpsed a small dreamcatcher Myrna had attached to the window shade, its three white feathers dangling above the bed. He knew grief was part of his process. He thought back to those first days after her death, to how utterly final everything felt. He had reminded himself that the sadness doesn't last forever when you honor your feelings and allow them to flow. Stay focused on the present because *NOW* is all we really have. He knew all the personal growth work he'd accomplished would see him through this dark time in his life. And sitting here now, even though it was still uncomfortable to look at her last photo, he was proud how quickly he had moved through his grief to a place of acceptance and peace.

Then, with the little energy he had left, he got up and began packing.

Only a few days after her call with Mel, Lynda found herself sitting on a too-hard chair, in a too-cold living room. She tried to smooth down the goosebumps as they crawled up and down her arms, pricking her skin. The shades were drawn against the sun and the only sounds were a squeaky ceiling fan punctuated by Wade's scribbling. Every few seconds the scribbling stopped, then started, then stopped again. She'd been waiting for ten minutes.

"I'm just checking to see if all the signatures are there," he said, glancing over at her from a small kitchen table. Lynda managed a polite smile, scrutinizing him as he fingered through the divorce papers. His face appeared moist and pasty, his forehead casting a grim sheen. She felt anxious and began to wonder if he was stalling. Then, as she studied him more closely, she realized he was hurting. He was losing something... a dream he'd once shared with her not too long ago. And even though she knew they weren't meant for one another, she still felt love for him. She didn't want him to hurt.

She felt his pain, and her heart ached for them both. They'd failed one another.

She stifled an impulse to reach out and comfort him. She remembered their counselor telling her that showing Wade affection was wrong because it was confusing for him. She needed to have clear boundaries.

Just then Wade stood up, the papers curled in his hand like a baton. "They're ready," he said, simply.

Mel's advice had worked.

The waiting was finally over.

CHAPTER THIRTY
SIGNS

It was an early weekday morning in mid-July when Mel stood in his daughter Melanie's kitchen watching the steam from a pot. A baby's bottle full of milk simmered in the middle of it. A blue, plastic banner exclaiming "Happy Birthday!" still hung on the wall above the dinette table. Other than that and the leftover birthday cake, no other signs of Joshie's boisterous first birthday party remained. Mel arrived in Minnesota the day before Joshie's birthday and was scheduled to be there five days before returning to Colorado.

As usual, he'd loved every minute, but he also found himself distracted by thoughts of Lynda and the dual jolt of elation and apprehension they left in their wake. He met Myrna at thirteen, and they married at nineteen. He never experienced dating as an adult, much less in these modern times. It all felt surreal.

Their well-established friendship comforted him, for he suspected he'd be pretty useless if he had to figure out how to date a total stranger. Lynda was different. He was comfortable with her. And his affection and familiarity anchored him, allowing him to drift through uncharted territory.

At completely random moments, he found himself wondering what her hair smelled like, if she liked red or white wine, or which side of the bed she slept on. He pictured her standing at her stove as she cooked a delicious dinner for her kids, and he wondered if it might be spaghetti or steak. He fantasized, too, imagining her smile at something he did or said. And he remembered how her skin waxed pearl-like under the moon on July fourth.

While he delighted in these musings, when he thought about the *reality* of a romantic relationship with Lynda, he had one concern. *I don't want to complicate her life.* She was going through her split with Wade. Did she need more time to grieve that loss?

His ring-side seat at the edges of Lynda and Wade's painful relationship had been a challenge to remain neutral. He and Myrna even counseled the couple several times, and regardless of the nature of their disagreements, if Lynda wanted to save her relationship with Wade, that's what he wanted too. First and foremost in Mel's mind was the happiness of the individuals, and he kept his own judgement out of it. Now, he suspected that he didn't truly know how painful things had been for her. Even though they'd been friends for years, they didn't tell one another everything. And, he wanted more than anything to ask her, to know, to move beyond the intimacy they'd established as friends.

The intensity of his interest struck him as ridiculous, and a part of him wondered if he felt more strongly than he should. Still, he couldn't deny his growing desire to be someone who gave her something more, if even for a moment. The two weeks until they'd see each other shimmered in front of him like a horizon, one he traveled into and towards, without knowing the final destination.

He recalled the teachings of *Ask and It Is Given*, words he took to heart because they resonated with his beliefs and teachings. The book was about God, or source energy, and how everyone embodied some of that energy, that is was possible to practice directing this energy as a joyful creator. If this was true, he reasoned, his future was his to create. Clearly, he wasn't finished teaching or learning, or for that matter, loving. And wasn't love the greatest teacher of all?

When he had finished creating his Ideal Partner list, he had stated to the universe, *If you want me in another relationship, God, here's my order.* He hadn't heard or intuited a response but trusted that he had been heard. The memory of that moment felt like pure oxygen as he grabbed the bottle and headed to the living room to feed the baby. Then, he heard a muffled voice that seemed to come from somewhere in the house.

Startled, he took a step toward the bedroom to see if the voice was coming from a radio. Finding only silence, he looked toward the entryway to see if someone might be at the door. No one.

He stood erect in the living room like someone poised to catch a mouse and waited to see if the voice would call out again. He tried to ignore the irrational fear that began to edge his bewilderment.

Could someone be in the house?

Then the voice said, "Hello, Mel?" from the corner of the living room. He made his way towards it and looked down. There, on a side table, sat his cellphone. Still confused, but understanding the voice was coming from his phone, he answered it.

"Hello?" he asked. His phone hadn't even rung. Then, he heard Lynda's voice.

"You called?" she answered, taken aback by his response.

"I called?" he stammered. "No, I just heard your voice . . . my phone didn't even ring."

Lynda paused to puzzle it out. She'd been sitting at her computer checking email and getting ready for work when her phone rang. But when she'd answered, no one was there.

"Well, I didn't call you, either," she said, disoriented. "My phone rang, so I answered it. Look at your phone and see what your call log says." She glanced at her phone. "Mine shows an incoming call from you."

Mel looked and saw the arrow that signaled he'd made an outgoing call to her. "This is just crazy . . . but you're right. It says *I* called *you*. But I haven't touched my phone all morning. I've been taking care of Joshie." They both fell silent.

"Well, that's weird," Lynda said. Mel agreed, feeling it had to be more than simple coincidence.

"I guess we're supposed to talk?" she asked.

"Yeah, it sure does seem like someone wants us to talk, doesn't it?" Mel stared at his phone, still perplexed at its autonomy.

Lynda had read that souls no longer trapped in the human body could move their energy through electronics. Who might be trying to reach them?

She turned away from her emails and said, "Well, let's talk."

So, that's exactly what they did.

She told Mel that Brandy and Nick were still dating. Recently, they'd woken her up in the middle of the night playing a children's game Brandy had since she was younger, something Lynda found adorable... and ridiculous.

He told her how Melanie had buzzed her hair and was as passionate and outspoken as ever. Currently, she had two dogs, two cats, and a chinchilla. And Joshie was great, as evidenced by his vigorous toss of an empty bottle across the room.

Underneath the chitchat, as morning light slanted through her window, Lynda noticed that Mel sounded different. For the first time since the fourth of July, she knew he wanted to talk to her.

No, that he was excited to talk to her.

The uncertainty of the past week had been hard on her. Even though their dinner was still on, the distance and time lag between had been frustrating.

She'd talked to Mel once or twice since making the dinner date, but the conversations had been brief and unmemorable, leaving her wondering. She felt more doubtful than ever. She'd convinced herself that it would be impossible to read him, or the situation, until she saw him in person. This placed her firmly in a kind of limbo she was unsure she wanted to tolerate. A few times, she'd even resolved not to pursue it, whatever "it" was. It just felt too agonizing, too hazy, too risky. Her concern over any potential fallout from a failed dating attempt discouraged her most of all. She was afraid of harming their friendship, and of what other people might think. But as she heard him tell her, "I think I'm going to visit some National Parks next week," she felt sure this conversation felt like the breakthrough she needed.

It *felt like a sign.*

"Which ones?" Lynda asked lightly.

"Which Parks? Yellowstone. Salt Lake. Maybe one or two others."

"Wow, I've never been to that part of the country," she said. She thought of the grandeur that would soon surround him. As a sense of total freedom overcame her, she added, "I wish I could be there."

Mel liked that. "I wish you could, too," he agreed, thinking about nothing except how far away she felt in this moment. "It would be really nice to see you."

The spirit of their conversations deepened over the next couple of weeks. Mel zig-zagged around the West while Lynda remained in Tampa. As they crossed divides of time and distance, the tightrope stretching between intimacy and uncertainty pulled taut. In their attempt to meet in the middle, they lost and regained balance. They began to look forward to seeing one another's name on their cellphones. They suffered and exalted. They left messages and returned calls. Secretly, they both came to regard the looming August third dinner as a kind of finish line, one that might close the loop between the present and the future, between desire and satisfaction.

They both felt more certain that something special, something new and different, was happening. And the dinner date would be the true litmus test. What they surprisingly did not talk about was what did or didn't happen on July fourth.

Each time they spoke, Lynda waited for an opening, for the right time to bring it up, but she always backed down. Its mention would simply reveal an admission that still felt too sensitive and raw.

The only time she came close was while Mel was in Jackson Hole, and she called with the intention of absolutely, one hundred percent talking about the fourth of July. She was, she told herself before picking up the phone, *going to do it this time*. So they made excruciating small talk while Mel stood on a street corner and Lynda waited for the perfect moment.

They talked about the weather in Jackson Hole, blue skies with afternoon chance of showers. They talked about Mel's hike that morning. and about the August RYL class in Tampa, the day after their dinner date. They talked about how Lynda had filed her divorce papers, and how incredible she found it that such a massive predicament could be so efficiently concluded. They cracked little jokes and amused one another. They even talked about "destiny," such as Mel's desire for another partner, and how he was ready if it was meant to be.

And then, right as Lynda readied herself to open up, Mel innocently said, "You just never know what the universe has in store. I'm watching a woman cross the street right now, and I'm asking myself, could she be the one?"

Lynda's cheeks flushed with embarrassment at having nearly spilled her truth to him right as he was hypothetically considering another woman. She struggled to make sense of his words but didn't know him well enough to understand how an intrinsic shyness sometimes made him awkward. She wondered if this was his way of trying to conceal his feelings for her. Or, maybe it was a way of drawing her out, inviting her to broach the subject of their budding romance. Whatever the case, she lost her resolve.

She hoped she'd be able to discern exactly how he felt when he returned to Tampa.

The weekend before Mel returned to Florida, it was early evening as Mel pulled the Loft into a rest stop in Idaho and cut the engine. He was headed to Salt Lake, where he planned to base the Loft while he flew back to Tampa. He glanced at his planner in the passenger seat. Then he reached over, picked it up, pulled a piece of paper out, and unfolded it. It was his Ideal Partner list.

His nerves somersaulted as he thought about his dinner with Lynda only a few days away. They hadn't talked in a couple of days and while something in their conversations made him "almost" sure she felt the same way he did, he still wasn't certain. How could he be, when so much remained unspoken? He'd wanted to say something a few times, but he couldn't figure out how to broach the subject or worse, how to handle it if the conversation turned awkward. He stared through the Loft's huge, streaky windshield at a grassy field and weighed his options.

The real problem was figuring out how to conduct himself at dinner. And to figure that out, he needed to know if he was going to a romantic dinner or not.

A pang of astonishment at his current circumstances bolted through his body, as it often did. Was he really going to have a *dinner date* with Lynda? He asked himself silently for the hundredth time, *Lynda? Really?* It was almost too much.

But his disbelief and uncertainty hadn't fully surfaced until now. If anything, it had only greased the roller coaster of excitement and anticipation he'd concealed from everyone over the past month. It had been his delicious secret. Now, the proverbial rubber was hitting the proverbial road. Uncertainty, even the thrilling chemical kind he never dreamed he'd actually have a second chance at, wasn't going to cut it. It was time for knowledge.

It was time to talk to Lynda about their connection.

Still holding his list, he picked his cell phone up and dialed her number.

CHAPTER THIRTY-ONE
DEEP DOWN

His silent, incredulous voice started again. *Am I really going to do this?* He pushed himself through it. He had to know how to respond when she opened that door.

"Hey, Mel," he heard Lynda say over the phone. It was ten o'clock at night in Tampa. She sounded a little sleepy. And completely effortless.

"Hello, Lynda," he replied. His nerves almost made him feel like he was outside of his body. "I'm heading into Salt Lake City and I . . . just wanted to say hi. Is it too late?"

"No, not at all." Lynda had already tucked herself in and was resting comfortably. "Didn't you say you were going to the lake?" Salt Lake City took its name from the Great Salt Lake, a massive remnant from an ancient ice age. He'd read the lake was too salty to support life.

"I'm planning on hitting the lake's beach and going for a swim – or float, as the case may be."

"It has a *beach*?" Lynda couldn't quite reconcile this with the Tampa beaches she'd grown up with.

"Yeah, I think they put sand out to make a beach, but it's pretty much a beach. And the water has more salt than the ocean so you don't sink. You can just float on top." Lynda pictured Mel floating motionless in a primordial, watery expanse. The image seemed symbolic. "Listen, I was wondering . . ." Mel stopped. He couldn't believe how nervous he felt. His words were sticking in his throat again.

"You were wondering?" Lynda said, but she already sensed what he was going to say. She could feel it. The clarity she'd been yearning for was finally at hand.

"Well, do you remember when we were on the beach on July fourth?" He imbued the word *we* with a tender emphasis Lynda didn't fail to miss. She wanted to make this easy for both of them.

"I remember we held hands," she affirmed.

They paused, each recalling their memories of that night. Mel remembered light, all kinds of light. In the sky and on her skin and the fathomless depth of her eyes. Lynda remembered the doped-up sensations in her body, how she spent the night in a titter of nervous intoxication. As she waited for his response, she felt it again.

Of course, she'd felt it before with other men, but this felt different. Safe. She knew he wouldn't be asking her if he didn't feel the same way.

"And did you feel anything?" he asked in a hushed voice.

"Yes, I did. What about you . . . did you feel anything?" Relief washed through her. She almost didn't even need to hear the answer. It felt so good to just talk about it.

Then he admitted, "I did, too." Mel rejoiced inwardly. *This is real. She was there with me.* He watched two blonde children bouncing up the field, a weary looking woman wrangling a tote bag behind them. Now, he'd know something about what to expect for their dinner date. But he needed more. "Well," he added, "what do you think?"

"I think . . . on one hand I feel great." She doodled in the margins of a crossword puzzle. "We're such great friends that I think it could work but then . . . what if it doesn't? What if we lose our friendship." It wasn't a question.

Mel considered this. He hadn't thought about it like that, but she was right. There was a lot at stake. He didn't want to do anything that would jeopardize their friendship. Then he found himself asking a question he'd asked hundreds of times within the sanctum of the course room, after people poured out their hearts and souls, not sure what they wanted but knowing they wanted more.

"What would it take for you to be sure?" he asked.

Lynda's answer rose from her gut. All she needed was to be in his presence. She'd known this all along. She felt her answer dangle, dropping like a penny into a deep, dark wishing well.

"I'll know when I see you."

On the day before he returned to Tampa, Mel hung a right into Bridger Bay Beach's parking lot. The beach, part of Antelope Island State Park, was the next stop on what he called his "National Parks Tour." The summer heat and the proximity of Island Buffalo Restaurant combined to impart a tangy aroma of wetland brine, sushi, and tater tots. As he regarded the area, he wrinkled his nose and thought its strange salty smell much more ocean-y than the actual ocean. Bridger Bay featured the shoreline of Utah's Great Salt Lake, which rested only about five hundred feet away, to thank for its signature scent. He'd seen sweeping pictures of dramatic mounds of gray salt, big as Montreal's roadside snow piles, heaped on the lake's shore. But this little beach looked more like a flat marsh. And other than a few cars sitting abandoned in the parking lot and the screeching of gulls, the area was sparse and peaceful. Empty even.

As he stepped out of his car, he noticed his Ideal Partner list, which still sat folded on his planner in the passenger seat. He reflected on it, then looked out towards the water. For the first time in a while, he felt the tranquility of being alone. The sheer strangeness of his environment struck a serene note. He'd written the list several months ago from the depths of grief.

But it had been a grief with hope. Hope for a new life, a life with love.

As extraordinary as it seemed, maybe his prayer was being answered.

This was the thought in his mind as he started towards the lake, towel in hand. The smell grew more pungent as he got closer, and he began to notice large, flat pebbles dotting the sand like coins. He passed through a whir of tiny flies that whizzed down the shore as far as his eye could see. Even though the air was still and muggy, small waves lapped over his sandaled feet as he began treading into the shin-high water.

He began searching for a spot deep enough to float.

He walked in the lake for what seemed like an eternity, towards a center point he couldn't discern. Surrounded by such an expanse, his mind emptied itself of thoughts, even those of prayer. All the emotions and experiences of the past four months blurred together. It all felt monolithic. So very big. But what once threatened to engulf him now stood twinned by the immensity of his travels, of things he traveled under and over, things that entered his dreams and were now a part of him. He'd hiked the serrated balconies of the Grand Tetons, leveled gazes with elk, mule deer, and bison, descended into the sleepy haze of Red Rocks Canyon. And he'd done it all alone. The scale of all his experiences, visible and invisible, dazzled him until he felt reduced to something purely elemental, like the salt of the water.

He'd changed.

He'd wandered – his only lifelines his memories and faith in his cherished RYL practices. He knew he'd never be completely over Myrna's loss, but he'd healed enough to feel alive again, to begin to understand who he'd be after he'd lived through his worst nightmare. Tragedy struck everyone. Now he knew he'd become stronger for it, someone who lived in a world where prayers were still answered, where miracles could still happen.

He bent down and cupped water in both hands, letting it drain away as he took in the distant mountains rimming the lake. Then he sunk into the water and let his body float, his arms drifting away from him.

He didn't know what was ahead for himself or Lynda. He didn't know whether she'd ever feel "sure" or whether he'd ever truly have a second chance at love. He just knew how he felt – an overwhelming sense of complete and utter surrender. His only thought, as he squinted into the sun, was about how bright it all was, about how clean and good life could be.

CHAPTER THIRTY-TWO

RENDEVOUS

"Would you like to share an appetizer?" Cindy asked Mel from across the table. "I know you love the fresh rolls." Mel unfolded the menu and held it like a screen between them. He'd arrived from Salt Lake earlier that afternoon, and while he'd done a pretty good job containing his euphoria, the prospect of seeing Lynda at the assistant meeting after dinner made him giddier by the minute. Still, he hadn't told anyone about Lynda and didn't want to give anything away, not even to Cindy.

"No, thank you," he said clearing his throat. "I'm really not that hungry tonight." He noticed Cindy's trademark Cheshire grin as a question seemed to dawn in her hazel eyes. Her gaze turned probing, knowing even. He realized that after ten years of being friends and business partners, she had great intuition and could sense when something was up. But that didn't mean he wanted to talk about it. At least not yet. He wasn't as concerned with what she'd think as with the fact that he didn't know what was going on himself.

"What's going on?" Cindy asked. "You seem different...on edge or something."

"I guess I'm just excited to be home, especially to be with RYL family tonight."

"Sure," she agreed. "I imagine it gets lonely being out on the road." Their waitress unloaded water, two glasses of wine, and a complimentary plate of sticky buns.

Cindy spread her napkin in her lap with beautifully manicured hands and placed one of the sweet rolls on her plate before asking another question.

"So, you mentioned you didn't need a ride back to my place after the meeting. Whose car are you using?" She usually shared her car with him, so he could get around Tampa, but this time, he'd arranged to borrow Lynda's extra car. A part of him had been hoping Cindy wouldn't ask about this. He took a sip of water.

"Well, it just so happens that Lynda has a car I can borrow while I'm here. I didn't want to put you out." He hoped this explanation would satisfy her curiosity. Cindy continued.

"Put me out? You know you're always welcome to borrow my car."

"I know," he agreed mildly. "But Lynda offered, and I thought 'why not?'" Cindy looked puzzled.

"Lynda Saffell?"

"Mm-hmm."

Cindy sipped her wine slowly, thoughtfully.

"Well, that was nice of her ... have you all been talking a lot?" Cindy knew that grads often took advantage of his open-door policy, but she wasn't always aware of the deeper friendships that developed because she rarely attended RYL social gatherings. Still, her question struck him as if she were fishing for information. He figured she was probably just being curious.

"Not much more than usual. We've talked a few times over the past few weeks. Mostly, she's needed help around Wade." Cindy bit into her sticky bun, nodding.

"Didn't they call off their engagement?"

"Yes, and he's not making it easy for her." Mel watched the waitress set his dinner in front of him. He was used to keeping

Cindy updated in this way, but he still felt resistant to talking about Lynda.

"Well, breakups can get complicated." Cindy had recently ended her marriage, so he knew she understood all too well. "I hope she's handling it well." As Mel ate his fried rice, he wondered why everything she said tonight sounded like a question.

"Actually, she's feeling great. She has found acceptance and found more clarity." Cindy smiled.

"So," she said breezily, changing the subject. "What are the numbers like this weekend?" Mel told her he'd enrolled ten students so far.

"And two unconfirmed. It looks like we have about forty assistants signed up to help out."

"Did you hear from Carolann?" Cindy usually recruited one or two students per month, and Carolann was Cindy's student.

"I did and she's all set to go."

Later that evening, Lynda walked past a regiment of palm trees and stepped through the breezy door of a large building, Billy and Brandy trailing behind her. A kelly green sign that read "Girl Scouts of West Central Florida" greeted her inside. She'd been here so many times for RYL classes, but this time, all the colors appeared more saturated, the glass windows clearer, as if she was seeing it all for the first time. Her heart skipped as she thought of Mel.

The last time they spoke, she told him that she'd know how she felt when she saw him. But as she walked towards the course room, she embraced the fact that she already carried her knowing with her, like a secret yearning to be told.

Lynda grinned at a girl scout staffer working late and headed down the hallway to the course room. Boisterous assistants gathered in small groups of three and four, busying themselves with the usual prep work, but mostly enjoying one another's company. As she scanned the spacious, meeting room looking for Mel, she caught the eyes of several people who flashed warm smiles in her direction. Normally, she would stop and chat, but she couldn't think of anything but finding Mel somewhere in the room.

She noticed a second, darkened room past the one she was in. It was usually sectioned off by a folding partition, but someone had drawn the partition open like a curtain, doubling the course room's area. With the exception of a few tables and stacks of chairs, it was empty. One shadowy figure leaned against the far wall, deep in a phone conversation.

It was him.

CHAPTER THIRTY-THREE
NOT LEAVING YOU GO

Buying time, Lynda joined a small huddle of women, exchanging hugs with each of them. As soon as she saw him end his call and start to walk towards her, she left the circle to meet him.

Churning with emotion, she felt magnetized toward him, into everything she ever wanted, into trusting her heart. When they drew together, she hugged him and closed her eyes, feeling his arms reach around and embrace her, obliterating all the distance and doubt of the past month. As she began to let go of the embrace, he pulled her into him again, holding her body against his.

He leaned down towards her ear, grazing her skin as he murmured, "I'm not leaving you go until you are sure."

Lynda knew that "leaving you go" was the Canadian equivalent of "letting you go." She felt the strange phrase slip into her awareness like a key, unlocking the only words possible for her in that moment. Words beautiful and simple.

"I'm sure," she said as she heard the words echo within her. *I'm sure, I'm sure, I'm sure, I'm sure . . .*

Around them, the space expanded like an oasis, all the voices and activity from the adjacent room blurring into silence and stars. If anyone was watching them, neither took notice.

After a moment he asked, "Do you want to go somewhere after the meeting . . . to talk about all this?" She looked up at him. His blue eyes appeared warm and tender, his face handsome and robust. She recalled him suggesting they meet when he returned to Tampa so she could read his mysterious list. She felt impossibly happy.

"That would be great," she managed to say as they reluctantly broke their embrace.

Outside, palm tree fronds ruffled at the tops of the windows as Mel went to gather his paperwork for the meeting, and Lynda re-joined the larger group. She couldn't help but sense her own glow, beaming as intensely as a searchlight whenever she looked in his direction. She'd never been very good at hiding her feelings and wasn't convinced she needed to. She felt herself drawn back into the circle of women she'd been chatting with before.

The start of a new course was always exciting, and each of the women, all in their forties and fifties, beamed their unique smiles. At six feet, Cindy towered over all of them, resplendent in her glossy elegance. Though she enjoyed feminine touches, Lynda was more comfortable in jeans, preferring a more natural look. Cindy's impeccable appearance never ceased to amaze her.

Sandy, Cindy's twin sister, flanked Cindy on the right, a quiet, lunar smile blooming on her face.

Becky was also there, beaming her characteristic, genuine grin that reached her warm Romanian eyes. It was the only adornment she needed.

As the three women welcomed Lynda into the fold, their combined presence felt comforting, abundant, and loving.

"I'm so glad you're here this month," Cindy said to Lynda, her arm around Sandy's waist. Then she nodded at Sandy and added, "Just like I'm glad to see this one." Sandy, a head shorter than Cindy, glanced up at her sister, an adoring gleam in her eye. As they chatted, Mel called the meeting to order.

The women began to break away to take their seats, leaving Cindy and Lynda behind. Cindy stared knowingly at Lynda from behind her wide smile.

Then she asked, "So, how's your new relationship?" as if she shared a little secret.

A look of surprise flashed across Lynda's face. It was all so completely new, and she felt herself thrown off balance. She hadn't considered the possibility that Mel may have discussed their relationship with Cindy.

"He told you?" Lynda stammered, confused.

Cindy affirmed with a wink, lengthened her toothy grin, and went to take her seat.

The assistant meeting was starting.

A group of about twenty assistants sat quietly in the now dimmed room while Lynda walked a slow circle. A scatter of white papers lay face down on the floor. Each one belonged to an incoming student. On it, the students had written their goals, hopes, fears, dreams.

As she neared each one, she tried to sense its energy. Sometimes the energy felt like a visceral tug, others like a thought or question. She scanned the papers, not with her eyes but with her heart. After a few moments, she felt drawn to one, and she knew it was the one that called to her. She picked it up, held it to her chest, and listened with her heart. She turned it over to read it and saw a man's name.

When he arrived for the course, she would be his "angel."

This magical exercise, in which an assistant chooses a student to guide and help throughout the weekend, was an RYL ritual. And it was one of Lynda's favorites because it not only taught her to listen to her intuition, but it affirmed it. Every time she chose a student to assist, she learned at some point during the weekend exactly *why* they'd been divinely "paired' together.

When she began this exercise tonight, she was unsure if she'd be able to focus on the moment. She'd felt so elated from finally connecting with Mel, while Cindy's comment had left her questioning. *If Mel told Cindy, who else did he tell?* But the exercise had actually grounded her, giving her what she needed to be present and find clarity.

On its surface, RYL was a psychology-based course. But the angel exercise was one of the ways it naturally merged into spirituality. "Angel-ing", as it was called, was based on the belief that people were energetically connected, that it was possible to discern and respond to a person when they weren't in the room, even when they were complete strangers.

Even, Lynda believed, *when they were no longer on this earth.*

CHAPTER THIRTY-FOUR

LIST NO.2

The moon sat golden and high as Lynda buckled herself in the passenger seat, and Mel headed towards the restaurant. She rolled the window down, slipping her palm into the damp, fragrant air.

The angel exercise had dispersed the shadow of confusion cast by Cindy. True, Lynda wouldn't have pegged Cindy as the person Mel would confide in this early. Then again, she didn't know everything about him, especially now that their relationship was changing so fast.

She regarded him as he drove. Even though she'd worried about their age difference, his hair shone thick, silver, and glossy. His build was healthy and athletic, and he had a casual, youthful look about him, dressed in jeans and an unassuming blue polo shirt. She turned back to the window, letting the scenery flow by like a silent movie.

He was now both intimate and unfamiliar, a good friend who'd been like a big brother was now suddenly captivating and new. It was a heady sensation. She wanted to ask him every kind of question, to glut on the story of his life, to let love's rush overtake her. But a small, ringing part of her also questioned herself. It was the voice of doubt, the one that never believed she could actually have the life she desired or dreamt of. *Am I good enough for him? Could I actually be in love? Could it really be this easy?*

Yes, she thought as Tampa's sprawl spun by, this was definitely a journey into unexplored territory.

As she glanced over at him, an amused grin lit his face, piquing her curiosity.

"What's that smile about?" she asked playfully.

"I was remembering Brandy and Nick's budding romance on July fourth." The fact that her daughter's new relationship had sparked nearly the same time as Lynda and Mel's had was sweet synchronicity. And she was mindful that talk about the kids might just as easily apply to her and Mel. He pulled into the parking lot.

"It's been really exciting to watch their relationship unfold. I hope it continues to go well after she starts Florida State."

A boyish expression peeked through Mel's normally controlled manner. He put the car in park, glanced up meaningfully. "If it's meant to be, it will."

She agreed, rolling the window up as he reached in the backseat for his planner. He started to say something else but as their eyes met, their bodies, only inches apart, drew together. Then their kiss, sweet and inevitable, erased the world as it joined their two hearts.

A few minutes later they sat shoulder to shoulder in a cushioned booth talking softly. Stained glass ceiling lamps studded the dimness, the smell of grilled steak permeating the air. A bartender plunged silver scoops into ice bins, chatting over his shoulder with a man sitting high on a bar stool. Lynda, still off-balance from the kiss, felt her blood drum through her veins. She longed to read Mel's list and imagined the look of delight on his face when he discovered that she'd brought her own.

The growing intimacy between them was thick and palpable, and they smiled at the bartender as he approached to take their order. It was late but he reassured them.

"We'll be closing soon but I've got plenty to do. So, just relax and take your time. My name's Chuck." His agreeableness and willingness to let them stay after closing time underlined Lynda's sense of luck, of sheer fortune. Then she watched Mel pull a piece of paper from his planner. He unfolded it carefully and placed it on the table between them, smoothing it out with his hands. Lynda registered a mysterious, tectonic shift as she gazed at his list.

Till now, they'd shared a few phone calls, held hands a couple times, and hugged at the assistant meeting. But as she looked at the list, she knew the relationship was jumping to a level she hadn't expected.

She unzipped her purse, reached in, took out her list, and placed it beside his. Their two lists, like everything else on the table, seemed to sparkle under the light. A look of mild confusion swept over his face as he examined them.

"What's this?" he asked.

"It's my Ideal Partner list. I wrote it after you told me about yours."

"You didn't tell me about this!" He was genuinely surprised. She smiled mischievously, shrugging.

"Well, I was saving it. I didn't really know what for, but I guess it was for tonight."

Lynda leaned over his list and began to read. It was long, every line of the legal-sized paper occupied. Its marked similarity to her own struck her immediately.

Must have chemistry. Nonsmoker. Affectionate. Loves animals. Loves the outdoors. Loves sports. Loves to travel (RV). Spiritual, not religious. Is part of the RYL community . . .

"Wow, I have that one, too," she said, sipping her wine and pointing at *Young at heart.* Mel nodded as he read her list, a look of amazement dawning over his face.

"And this and this and this." *Health conscious. Is financially independent. Loves to laugh.* "It's almost like they're the same lists," he exclaimed with disbelief, as if he'd just stumbled onto buried treasure.

"Mmmm," Lynda agreed enthusiastically. "Except this one." She gestured to an item on her list. *Age range between 35 and 55.*

"Well, I can assure you I am the world's oldest teenager. You'll see," he joked, brandishing his wine glass playfully. Would she? Would she see? This was all going so fast. It felt a little scary. She didn't trust herself as much as she wished. She'd made what felt like too many bad decisions in love, let herself get needlessly carried away. Believed people when she should've known better. Looked away when she should've asked questions. Settled.

But this? This felt impossibly easy. And undeniably, inexplicably right. Their lists, especially when read together, seemed to reinforce what her heart already knew. But there was something more.

"When did you make this list, again?" Lynda asked.

"April tenth. I remember it like it was yesterday." A rushing synchronicity, like a cool jolt lightning, cascaded through Lynda's body. It triggered the memory of the day she stood in her foyer and stood her ground with Wade. He'd slammed the door. She looked at Mel.

"That was only one day after I called off the wedding with Wade." They stared at one another, shaking their heads in wonder and considering quietly.

What did it all mean?

Lynda leaned into Mel's neck and chuckled, her hair grazing his neck.

Mel, as if close to cracking a code with the lists as the key, repeated an RYL teaching she'd heard him say many times over the years. *What we believe is what we create.*

She'd always wanted to believe that, to *live* it, but sitting here, looking at the lists, she finally did.

An old, tattered anguish, her own miserable teaching began to unravel. *If it seems too good to be true, it is.* That's not what she wanted to believe anymore. Not now, not ever. Mel, the lists, the wine. They seemed to melt the years of cynicism and hopelessness of her old belief. She knew that almost everyone carried it in some form, but now, for her at least, it would rearrange itself into the only truth that mattered.

In this moment, she trusted that Life was on her side.

"I have to tell you, Lynda," Mel said quietly. "The word that keeps coming up for me is *compatible*. We've known each other for six years. I mean, we're not strangers." She listened intently, to Mel's silences as much as his words. "I wrote this list in April. Myrna was gone. I don't even know why I did it except that I knew my life wasn't over. It couldn't be. So much was happening . . . and then you... and traveling around the country . . ."

He shook his head as a wave of compassion washed through Lynda as she heard Myrna's name. She remembered Myrna's face, how it looked before she got sick. Beautiful, kind, and wise. The smile lines around her brown eyes crinkled, her quiet strength. Lynda felt the sting of tears behind her eyes – from happiness and from sadness.

"You've been through so much. So much change," Lynda said, feeling keenly the inadequacy of her words.

"I just feel like we're sitting here and . . . these lists . . . I feel like we're making an agreement. Where do we go from here?"

"From here?" she asked, surprised. He took another sip of wine. The bar was now empty of everyone but him, Lynda, and Chuck. He gestured at the lists.

"Lynda, this tells me that we're literally on the same page. I can't explain it, and I don't understand it. But I'm trusting the process. And I also feel like I know you, because I do." He hesitated. "I feel ready to commit." Mel hadn't planned to say any of this. How could he have known the lists would be so similar, so miraculous?

Lynda cleared her throat, jarred and incredulous at such a strong word. "Commit?" she asked weakly. Mel, probably sensing he'd thrown her, measured his words.

"I feel like we already know each other, so it's not like we need to date. Because that's for getting to know someone. I'm ready to commit to seeing where this goes, taking it very . . . you know . . . seriously. And I don't want you to feel pressured. If that's not how you feel, I understand. But that's what's present for me in this moment."

Lynda marveled at his directness, his boldness. She'd seen it in the course room many times. She thought of how some men used hints, suggestions, and evasions to communicate. Never letting her get in front of them without controlling the stakes. Always keeping her guessing, playing a game. And here Mel was, talking about commitment and *meaning* it. Their first date wasn't even until tomorrow, but somehow his proposal made sense. If anyone else had said this, it would be a red flag. But it wasn't someone else. It was Mel. And as she thought about it, she had to agree with his logic. They knew one another too well to date casually.

"Well," she heard herself say, "I think that makes sense. We've been good friends for a long time. It would probably be silly to date casually. Actually, I'm not even sure how that would work. And the lists . . . they do show that we're really compatible. There's only, like, two things on my list that don't match yours." He gazed at her, uncertainty in his eyes.

"So, you're in?" he asked. At this, Lynda swept up her glass, nearly emptied of its cherry-rose wine.

"I'm in. I'm all in."

Lynda's List

Qualities of My Ideal Mate

Desires an Equal Partnership
Healthy Sense of Responsibility
Physically fit & enjoys exercise & working out
Positive self-image
Positive outlook on life
Loves children & loves my children
Loves women / Healthy relationship with his mother
Good sense of humor
Spiritual Awareness and seeks spiritual growth
Affectionate, likes to hug & cuddle
Faithful and devoted
Honest
Emotionally Open
Dependable + trustworthy
Respects individuality & differences in me and other people
Enjoys his work / career is personally satisfying
Mentally challenging and stimulating
Assertive, able to make decisions / take action when necessary
Kind & friendly
Loves animals
Loves nature & spending time outdoors
Age - 35-50
Earns $50,000 + annual
Shares domestic responsibilities
Passionate
Playful
Contributes to making the world a better place
Plans activities to do together

Has a fun circle of friends
Creative
In Love with me
Validates + respects others feelings & opinions
Good communication skills

Lynda's Ideal Partner list

CHAPTER THIRTY-FIVE
ECSTATIC SINGING MANTRAS

Mel awoke to a new reality. The pleasant daze that had immersed him for the past month was intact, but the thunderstruck, internal voice that had so often asked *Lynda? Really?* was replaced with *We're in a relationship!*

He shuffled around Cindy's empty house and put in a solid, if distracted, day's work at the dining room table, startled every now and then at his own astounded exclamation, *We're in a relationship!* He shook his head and checked his watch at least twenty times and dawdled with the cat when he got antsy. He visited three stores and lingered over shelves of red wine looking for the perfect bottle. *We're in a relationship!*

Unbidden, impressionistic visions bloomed in his mind. Lynda on the beach, a moon snagged in the clouds. The shock of platinum sparks falling like a fountain behind their linked hands. Pulling a cramped airplane tray over his lap in what he thought would be a private moment and feeling the nib of his pen scrawl the traits of his ideal partner. Lynda's traits. A phone ringing in the morning. A hush when he finally took her into his arms at the assistant meeting. The sound of their wine glasses clinking together, that last wash of wine. His glee was molten and bottomless. And by the time Lynda opened her door to welcome him, it had even erased the irritations of rush hour and soothed his nerves a little.

When she took the wine bottle from him and invited him in, her face looked fresh, salt-scrubbed and radiant, as if she'd just returned from a swim in the ocean. Her bangs sloped casually to the side as she ran her fingers through them. The earthy smell of a candle mingled with the bone rich scents of dinner wafting from the kitchen.

"Nice to see you. You look great," he said, hesitating for a moment before hugging her warmly. She seemed so relaxed as she smiled and examined the wine. "This looks good. It will go well with dinner." Her voice sounded stronger than usual – full and resonant. He became aware of that hidden part of him that felt terribly, boyishly shy. It was perhaps the oldest part of him, the one that spoke a little Yiddish, a little French, a lot of English. The one that asked Myrna on her first date, played street hockey in the falling snow, bought his first leather jacket.

"Speaking of dinner, it smells amazing."

"Let's go open it," she said, leading him in. He followed her through the dining room, passing the hallway to the kids' empty bedrooms. Soothing music drifted from the stereo. Dark, green countertops outlined her bold, white kitchen. Then she paused at a short bar lined with dining stools. "Pick some glasses out, whichever call to you," she said.

Mel was familiar with this hostess ritual, which was why he was already opening the cabinet full of quirky glassware. He was pulling two fat, long-stemmed glasses down when he heard Lynda laugh behind him.

"It's a little early to be laughing at me," he teased.

"Have you read this?" she exclaimed, still holding the wine bottle. Mel smiled knowingly, headed back to the bar.

"I thought you'd enjoy that," he said as she began reading the label out loud.

"Giddy pleasure, leaping grace . . . this red wine, blended from seven noble grape varietals, was crushed by the feet of sixty-nine beautiful women in the wee light of dawn one misty

October day. The nose is deeply perfumed with wild dewberries, Himalayan breeding musk, and horehound candy, while the flavors, so titillating they may only be disclosed in an Ecstatic Singing Mantra, will remain cloaked in silence until the bottle is uncorked."

"Lynda, are you ready for your ecstatic singing mantra?" Amused, she grabbed the wine tool and eased the cork clear of the bottle, a muffled pop sounding through the room.

"Well," she answered as he poured, "here's to the grapes of sixty-nine beautiful women." They toasted and she went to the stove and opened a box of pasta. Humor was one of the primary ways they'd always related to one another. It felt comfortable and allowed him to relax. But he couldn't crack jokes all night. He wondered what to talk about next.

"So, where are Brandy and Billy again?" It was all he could think to ask.

"At their dad's." Mel thought of his three kids when they were teenagers, imagined what it would be like to raise them by himself. Lynda seemed to make single parenting look easy. Still, he knew it hadn't been easy at all.

"So, it's mom's night off?"

"Yes, although that's not as important as it used to be. They're growing up."

"Well, I'm really glad to be here with you," he said quietly. "Just the two of us." He watched a mass of noodles slide into a steaming pot.

"I know," she said, setting a lid on the pot. "Pressure's off." Mel chuckled, then realized it was one of those earnest truths that masqueraded as a joke. She was serious.

"Really? Isn't that interesting? Explain."

Lynda paused, searching for the right words.

"We skipped the awkwardness of dating. That's something I've never done before. Now, we can just relax and get on with it. And," she added, "we don't have to wait anymore. I don't know about you, but July was kind of hard on me. All the uncertainty." Mel covered her hand with his.

"Thank you for waiting," he said. He felt emotional. He knew she couldn't totally grasp the significance of these words that Myrna once spoke to baby Joshie. He couldn't wait to share the story with Lynda.

He felt he had so much to say, about everything.

CHAPTER THIRTY-SIX
READY

A silky, half-eaten mound of herby egg noodles and beef slices melted in the middle of Mel's plate, infusing the room with warm notes. He and Lynda sat nestled in an intimate pocket at her dining room table. The wine glasses and candle flames winked, their scents weaving with those of dinner. Mel re-filled each wine glass a quarter full, set the bottle down softly. So far, the conversation had stitched together candid accounts of their workdays, thoughts on the upcoming course, and even, at one or two points, their mutual excitement and joy at the prospect of their new relationship. They also wondered when and how they should share that joy with their families.

"I don't think my kids will be surprised," Lynda told him, a rich shine in her voice.

"No? Well, I'm still a little surprised." He took a bite, savoring the tender flavors of the beef bourguignon.

"Brandy knows. I mentioned it a couple of weeks ago." This piqued Mel's curiosity. He raised his eyebrows. "We were standing right over there," Lynda said, nodding towards the living room, "and I remember saying, 'Brandy, I think I'm attracted to Mel!' She just thought about it for a second and then she ran with it."

"She didn't ask questions?" Lynda shook her head no.

"She told me that you weren't who she pictured me with, but if that's what made me happy, I should go for it." Mel chuckled.

"Reminds me a little of Melanie. One day, two or three months after her mother died, we were talking about everything, and she looked at me and said, "If you need to go out and get laid, Dad, it's OK with me." They laughed together before Mel hastily added, "But we weren't talking about you. She was just commenting in general."

"Were you shocked?"

"No. Melanie has always been very direct and outspoken. And that's how we are as a family. Myrna and I always wanted them to be open about how they felt." As he said this, Lynda, eyes starry and open, tilted towards him and rested her chin in her palm. His eyes tumbled from her ear, down the slope of her neck, to her collarbone. His heart swelled in renewed astonishment at his luck. At being in a relationship. At this strong, marvelous redhead gazing at him. Then, he felt the old shyness slip back in. He hadn't dated since he was thirteen. In fact, he'd never experienced dating as an adult like Lynda had. Suddenly feeling completely out of his depth, he sipped his wine, grew quiet.

"Well, maybe we should tell our families next week before you leave," she suggested. Mel considered. He'd be in town for a few days after the course ended. Then he'd fly back to Salt Lake City. They had exactly one week together, a time frame that struck him as woefully short.

"We could do that," he replied, forking the last bite into his mouth. Then he looked at Lynda's plate. Empty. Her wine glass, also nearly empty, floated in her hand. She shifted in her seat, laid her napkin on the table, looked at him.

"Would you like more?" she said, eyeing his empty plate.

"No, thank you." He rested his hands in his lap, trying not to appear as awkward as he felt.

"What do you say we head to the living room, then?"

In a cloud of euphoria, he grabbed the wine bottle and his glass and followed Lynda.

A plush, pumpkin-colored sofa formed a semicircle in the middle of the room. A stone fireplace marked the far wall and a large T.V. faced the sofa. Mel placed the bottle, now half-full, on the coffee table, sat down and watched Lynda flip the lights on. She wiggled her shoes off, turned the stereo on and joined him, tucking her hand into his. For a few moments, the sounds of the music rinsed over them. They made small talk, but soon the sounds of the radio show, like the ticking of a clock in a distant room, faded from hearing. Their bodies grew closer, forming their own grammar as they weaved in and out of conversation, until the weight of all the things unsaid became heavier than language. They punctuated both banter and silence with kisses. A forehead on a shoulder. A hand caressing a blue-jeaned knee.

As he kissed her, Mel marveled at how it felt simultaneously natural and peculiar. He was a planner. But of all the things he'd planned on, making out with Lynda was not one of them.

The drive through rush hour traffic so he'd be exactly five minutes early, yes. The wine, yes. Even the flirting and a smattering of kisses, perhaps. But this was a level of physical intimacy he never would've imagined. At some point, their bodies released from the press and they sat up, breathing still heavy. Most of the wine had disappeared and it was late.

"Well," she said, arranging a throw pillow behind her. "It's getting pretty late." She sounded regretful, as if she wished it wasn't.

"Mmmm," Mel agreed. He wondered if she was trying to get him to leave. His throat was dry. Then she asked him what his plan was.

"My plan?" he stammered.

"Like, for the rest of the night?"

"I'm just going back to Cindy's and preparing for class tomorrow, I suppose," he said truthfully. Lynda drained her glass and gazed at him, her expression alluring and frank.

"Would you like to stay here?" At this, Mel was pretty sure he might choke.

"Stay here? But Cindy is expecting me." As soon as he said it, he realized how hollow it was and regretted it. He'd much rather stay with Lynda than go back to Cindy's guest bedroom. In fact, the only reason his response might make any sense at all was because, however insignificant, it was true. It was the plan. And it felt safe. Since Myrna died, his routine had been to stay at Cindy's whenever he was in Tampa. He also worried how he'd explain where he was if he didn't show up. As he tried to think of a way to redeem his answer, a look of understanding dawned in Lynda's eyes.

"Well, just give her a call and let her know so she won't worry." Mel hesitated, caught in wondering if there was any plausible explanation he could offer. He hadn't told Cindy anything about Lynda and he didn't want to. Then again, he'd also drank some wine.

Maybe he shouldn't drive.

"Okay," he said, plucking his phone off the coffee table. Lynda left the room and returned with two glasses of water. He took a sip, dialed Cindy's number. "Hello," he said into the phone.

"Hi Mel. What's up?" Cindy asked. She sounded tired, and he felt sorry about calling her this late. He kept his tone even, nonchalant.

"Not much. I'm sorry to call you at this hour, but I just wanted to let you know that I've been out. And I've had a few glasses of wine." Silence. "And anyway, I think I should stay at my friend's house tonight."

"Oh?" he heard her say, genuine surprise in her voice.

"So, I'll be at the house tomorrow morning."

"I totally understand." Cindy sounded taken aback. Then she added, "You're doing the right thing." As he ended the call, he noticed Lynda watching him. He felt self-conscious again. Had she been watching him the entire time?

"Everything okay?" she asked.

"I think so." Then, she caressed his cheek, and they kissed again. After a few minutes, Mel, legs back under him, began unbuttoning her shirt. It was smooth and cool, like a flower petal. Wordless, he drew his hand low across her neckline. It was supple and flushed. He looked at her, a question forming in his eyes.

"Are you ready?" he asked simply.

"Yes," she whispered. Before he had a chance to respond, she rose and disappeared into the bedroom, leaving him on the couch.

He sat there frozen, overcome by a sensation of sinking.

He tried to will his legs to move but they wouldn't budge. The familiar shyness possessed him as he wondered *am I truly ready for this?* His forehead moistened as he stared down at his hands. He'd followed the night to a logical conclusion, even though it wasn't one he'd planned on. All the right moves, the best date, the perfect woman.

And here he was, feeling utterly unprepared for her. He felt ridiculous.

Lynda came out of her bedroom, confusion in her voice. "Are you coming?"

He planted his feet on the floor, unclasped his hands. Then he stood up, put one foot in front of the other, and followed her into the bedroom. As he shut the door behind him, he noticed the bedspread folded down, exposing shiny, red sheets.

Ready or not, he was in a relationship.

CHAPTER THIRTY-SEVEN
RESISTANCE OF THE HEART
AGAINST BUSINESS AS USUAL

Lynda arrived Friday evening at the course room with Brandy and Billy. This was their first time as assistants, and they were full of questions on the drive over. *Do we get to be angels this weekend? What happens when we meet the students? Will I know any of them?* There was a buzz of excitation as they made their way up the stairs and into the course room.

Looking around at her friends and community, Lynda was keenly aware her life had changed dramatically, and ironically, no one else in the room knew it. Her secret filled her so fully that she felt like she might burst. She couldn't wait to share her joy about her new relationship, but she also felt a little nervous. On some level, it would affect their lives too. How would they react?

They busied themselves by helping out with the details of setting up the room and preparing to welcome the new RYL students. As she pinned on her name tag, she thrilled at the thought of the students entering the course room, because Mel would be right behind them. Hoping to collect herself, she was headed towards the Ladies room when she bumped into another assistant, Lisa.

"Hey, Lynda what's new?" Lisa asked warmly. Lynda was aware that Lisa had a special bond with Mel and Myrna, and Lynda had her own friendship with Lisa as well. They had all shared many good times together over the years, and she was hopeful that Lisa would be happy to hear her news. It was Lynda's habit to be honest and open, and she couldn't deny that Mel *was* the newest thing in her life. Lynda bit her lip, a gleam in her eye.

"Well, you're not going to believe this . . . but Mel and I are in a relationship." Lisa's eyes widened, in an expression of happy shock. The secret was out.

"What? When did this happen?" Lisa exclaimed. The question was a little complicated to answer. Did it start on July fourth, at the restaurant with the lists, or at dinner?

"Just yesterday, I guess," she answered, beaming. She knew it might sound sudden, but it was her truth. She was too happy to keep it in, and didn't the course teach about openness and authenticity?

"Wow, I'm so happy for you both," Lisa gushed. She sounded sincere.

"Oh, thank you. I'm really happy about it, too. I can barely believe it myself." How could she explain how this was so much more than just another new relationship? She knew this was special, the one her heart had been searching for.

As she settled back in the course room to await the students, she felt flooded by a sense of relief. Carrying secrets burdened her, and she'd never been very good at it. It felt so good to share, especially with someone she trusted.

The students began filing into the room, looking like most students on their first night, probably like she did on her first night. Exhilarated, scared, and curious. Friday night was about creating safety in the room and getting familiar with the basic principles of the work. And she'd meet the student whom she'd be angel-ing. She couldn't wait.

After they closed for the evening, Lynda chatted briefly with other assistants, still feeling downright conspicuous in her happiness. A couple times, she'd caught someone glancing at her from across the room and found herself wondering if Lisa had shared the news with anyone. Mel had been absorbed in his work leading the evening's discussions, so she hadn't expected to connect with him much. As she said her last goodbyes and started towards the elevator at the end of the night, a distinctive, resonant voice called out behind her. It was Peggy, another good friend who occasionally co-taught the course with Mel. As an instructor, Peggy was part of a core group of people who were most invested in the program.

"Hey, Lynda, wait up!" Peggy called. Lynda stopped and waited for her to catch up, and they began walking out together. They chatted lightly before Peggy eyed her, leaned in, and offered congratulations.

"For what?" Lynda knew the answer to her own question as soon as the words came out of her mouth. Lisa had shared her news, and that was fine with her. She knew that if Peggy knew, many others in the core group probably did too. In her joy, she hadn't anticipated the ripple effect it might have. She and Mel hadn't *thought* at all about how they would tell the RYL community, they were too busy being happy together.

"About you and Mel. Lovebirds." Lynda thanked her with a hug, then headed to her car where Brandy and Billy were waiting. As they drove home, she noticed the moon hanging on the horizon – round, orange and low. A wave of exhaustion swept through her body, and she knew she'd sleep soundly tonight.

CHAPTER THIRTY-EIGHT
HIGH STANDARDS

It never failed to amaze her. Once she heard someone's heartfelt life story, it awakened her compassion, and it became almost impossible to dislike or judge them.

She was sitting in a circle of other assistants, rapt as two students struggled to redraw the borders of their romantic relationship. She knew it felt counter-intuitive to expose and resolve such personal challenges in community, but that's what made the RYL process powerful. Being real and visible transformed everyone – assistants, students, and instructors. It gave new meaning to "The truth will set you free."

All morning, she'd been so immersed in the coursework and her responsibilities as an angel that she hadn't had time to think about Mel, even though they were in the same room. And no one else had mentioned her new relationship. The only sign of her happiness was the radiance infusing her face.

At the end of the couple's session, everyone cleared the floor of chairs and encircled them. Music filled the room and they all began swaying together in another RYL ritual. Each student received a song to decompress from and to celebrate their work, and the entire group typically shared a group hug. This moment was one of Lynda's favorites.

As she felt the familiar duet wash over her, its lyrics resounded in her body. The singer's lilt, *"I don't know much, but I know I love you,"* resounded through the room, impossible to ignore. She hummed along with the song, a song of knowledge and lost dreams, of love clarified and forged in life's inevitable disappointments. Lost in the moment, she walked around the circle and up behind Mel, wrapping her arms around his waist.

His muscles tensed slightly at this "public" display of affection, but only for a moment. Making a conscious decision to surrender to the moment, he stopped being the instructor – on task and on purpose – and shifted from his head to his heart as he turned his body towards hers and relaxed into her embrace.

Whoever didn't know about them yet would know now.

After the embrace, and all through the next morning, her conversations were thick with well wishes and congratulations. Being able to be open about her life, especially with her RYL family, was her comfort zone and default. She unfolded like a flower in the sun, enjoying a peculiar sensation that was too-good-to-be-true but was, in fact, deliriously true.

But not everyone was comfortable with that truth, as she was about to learn.

Later during a break, Mel pulled Lynda aside and passed a message from Cindy. She wanted to speak with Lynda. Too elated to think anything of it, Lynda hurried to the adjacent room, which served as the dining room. She found Cindy tidying up the snack table.

"Well, hey there," Cindy said, her voice breezy. She gave Cindy a hug.

"Mel said you needed me?" At this question, Cindy smiled and threw some empty plastic cups in a large trash can.

"Yeah, let's go to the kitchen, though. It'll be quieter." She gestured towards the course room, where Mel was leading a meditation exercise. Lynda knew that most of the students were reclined on the floor with their eyes closed, letting the meditation wash over them.

Lynda and Cindy small-talked as they headed down the hall, eventually finding a plain, institutional looking dinette table to sit at. The kitchen counters were cluttered with urns, coffee filters, and large cans of coffee. Lynda thought about pouring herself a cup. As she was about to ask Cindy if she wanted one as well, Cindy offered her own congratulations.

"Lynda, I wanted to share how happy I am for you and Mel. It is quite something." Something in Lynda's brain clicked into place. This must've been why Cindy wanted to talk to her. Lynda had always looked up to Cindy, and it meant a lot that she'd take the time to pull her aside and express this privately.

"Oh, thank you so much," Lynda said. Cindy's lips spread in a smile and she folded her hands on the table in front of her.

"And, there's something else." Something in Cindy's tone put Lynda on guard.

"Oh?" Lynda asked.

"You have to remember that Mel and I, we have a certain position to uphold. A role to fill as community leaders." Lynda knew this, but she still didn't understand how her relationship affected his role as a leader. "And our personal lives can affect the course. While I'm happy about your new relationship, I feel it may have caused some distraction this weekend."

Lynda was aware of the mounting excitement among the community and enjoyed the atmosphere of celebration it added. But she was fairly certain the news hadn't impacted the students.

"I'm not sure I understand."

"I think you should've asked Mel's permission before you told the community about your new relationship." Lynda felt her face flush, the distinct sting of a reprimand rippling through her.

"His permission?"

"Yes, because we're held to a higher standard than everyone else. It's important that certain information be handled appropriately. Strategically."

"Oh," said Lynda. She respected Cindy and struggled to interpret her words. Though she still couldn't understand how her love life would cause drama or upset in a community committed to being authentic and open, it was the last thing she wanted. Was Cindy implying she should've hidden something?

"But it can't be undone, now. It's water under the bridge," Cindy reassured her. "It's just something to be mindful of." Lynda still felt confused.

"Okay, I guess I can understand that."

"You know, going forward." Lynda glanced down.

"Of course," she said.

They walked back to the course room, Lynda's confusion a glaring interruption in an otherwise joyful day.

During an afternoon break, she noticed Mel walking towards her holding a map. "I was thinking," he started, "about how I'm returning to Salt Lake City in a few days and won't be back until mid-September." That was nearly six weeks away.

"I know," she said, a little gloomy.

"Well, I think that's too long." He paused to let his words sink in. "Do you have any vacation time? I'll be driving the Loft to California and I thought we could meet somewhere along the way." Lynda brightened.

"I have a week of vacation saved up, actually." He sat down beside her and unfolded the map. She watched him plant the tip of his finger on Nevada.

"How about Vegas? It would be great for in-and-out flights."

"Vegas! I haven't been there for twenty years . . ." Lynda could scarcely believe it, but somehow life was getting even better. He didn't want to be apart from her for too long, and she felt valued and appreciated.

Stealing a few moments, they quietly plotted their rendez-vous. Then, they worked until dinner, when the course finally broke and most everyone met at a local pancake house to celebrate graduation.

Lynda snuck wine into the eatery in a coffee mug and found Mel. The mood was light-hearted, but she wanted to get his opinion on her conversation with Cindy. She hated second-guessing herself, but she needed to know if he agreed with Cindy. *Maybe he did wish that she'd asked his permission.* But as she reiterated their conversation, he grew more surprised, perplexed even. He listened quietly, took a sip from the mug, set it down firmly, and gazed at her.

"Firstly, I didn't know that's what Cindy wanted to discuss with you. And, there is absolutely no reason you need to ask my permission to share anything about your life." His voice sounded definitive, and relief flowed through her. He wasn't just consoling her, he was adamant. She regretted that Cindy disapproved of her behavior, because she respected Cindy. Were there others who felt the same, she wondered. She'd struggled with "other people's opinions" for much of her life, putting others' feelings ahead of her own. But in RYL, she'd learned to be "inner directed" and to trust her feelings. She wondered if he would agree.

"I had a feeling you'd say that," she joked, sipping from their mug, a smile in her voice. She didn't want to reveal that she'd almost felt . . . scolded. "So you don't think that it created a distraction in the course room?" she probed.

"Absolutely none," he repeated, shaking his head. "The students were served. If anyone was upset by our relationship, that's just their opinion. And remember, other people's opinions are none of our business!" Then he leaned over, whispering conspiratorially, "And anyway, we'll always have Vegas."

CHAPTER THIRTY-NINE
ANGEL'S WINDOW

The trail was short, only about a half mile to Angel's Window, and relatively flat. Shady ponderosa pines lined both sides of it as Mel hiked towards its end, an exposed overlook. A cool, sweet-smelling canyon breeze ruffled the branches. He'd been at the Grand Canyon a couple of days. From here, he'd head north to Vegas. And Lynda. But for now, he walked towards Angel's Window, a colossal rock landmark located on the canyon's sparsely visited North Rim.

His hiking boots fell softly on packed earth as he neared a small clearing. From there, he spotted the landmark, as it jutted out over the abyss, forming a dramatic overhang. Mel zoomed his camera lens on it. The vivid sky and bright clouds visible through a large hole in the massive rock was the reason people called it Angel's Window.

He left the clearing and continued along the path, halting only to fetch a handful of day-old trail mix from his backpack. He quickly reached the trail's end which led onto the top of Angel's Window. When looked at squarely, it might appear like a narrow airplane runway hanging in the stratosphere, or a mile-long dock over an ocean. Then he took his first steps on the ceiling of the sky.

The metal railings of a barrier fence appeared to thrust randomly in different directions, like a piece of absurdist art. The air lost its sweet, earthy tinge, and became Zen-like and clear, inspiring the cool sensation of freshly fallen snow. The South Rim swept in front of him, peeling its patterned, sun-infused stone backwards to a hazy horizon. He paused, rested his hands on the railing. Three miles below, the Colorado River chiseled a green, meandering line.

As the sun illuminated a thousand russet and gold hues, he grew speechless. He wasn't a young man and yet here, surrounded by millions of years of earth's history, he was unthinkably young. He recalled the sound of Lynda's voice, which came to him easily now, since they'd talked on the phone every night since he'd left Tampa. With each conversation, he felt more solid, more real, as if he were returning to his body. Perhaps after Myrna died, some tiny part of himself he didn't know he was missing had departed with her. Or, perhaps she just anchored that part of him, and without her, it floated, a bird in the sky. Now, it was being sung back to itself.

Each night, he listened to Lynda talk about everything. He talked, too, but mostly he just wanted to listen to her voice. He would do that for as long as possible until she was ready to go to sleep. Maybe she'd close her eyes, pull the bedspread up. Maybe he'd hear the faint sound of her breathing and he'd lean in. Then he'd recite these words, very slowly. "Today is over. I did the best I could. I'm grateful for today and now it's time to rest my body and my mind."

Then he'd pause and add, "I love you, MP1." MP1 stood for "My Precious One," the nickname Lynda's grandmother gave her when she was a little girl.

How could he love her so much already?

Since July fourth, they'd only spent a few days together. And yet, here it was, love as substantial as the canyons, as the rock he stood on.

Remarkable as the sky.

Just then, a fellow tourist in a red ball cap walked past and waved hello. Mel waved back, smiled, and followed him to the edge. Mel uncased his camera and began pointing it in various directions, trying to focus it. A few moments went by before he lowered it, looked out, and stared. The camera's panoramic setting was insufficient, not nearly enough to capture the wonderment he was witnessing. He fiddled a little more, then watched the man leaning over the railing gaping at the view, just like he was. Both of their cameras hung uselessly from their necks.

"How am I supposed to capture all this in a four by six?" Mel asked the man as he gestured to the landscape. The man chuckled and shrugged.

"Beats me," he said.

Mel zipped up his camera case. "If people want to see this beauty, they've just got to be here."

Mel arrived in Las Vegas ahead of Lynda to scope things out and prepare the Loft. Wanting to make the most of their time together, he planned the trip meticulously. Then, two days before she was scheduled to arrive, he received news that shook him to the core.

He'd spent the afternoon in a phone conference with the August RYL students. They'd gathered for the traditional follow-up party and many of the assistants, including Lynda, were present. He still had to suppress a thrill whenever he heard her voice sparkling over his speakerphone.

He'd worked with Myrna, but they'd been married for over forty years. They'd had their "new relationship" energy as teenagers. By the time RYL rolled around, it had long been replaced by an established bond forged over decades.

Yet he maintained his composure by wearing his "instructor hat" facilitating the meeting. He knew he'd get to talk to Lynda later during their nightly phone marathon. He couldn't wait. So, he was surprised when, earlier than usual, she called. But her voice sounded nothing like herself. It was clipped, constricted, strained.

"Mel, are you there? I don't know what's wrong. I'm driving home from the follow-up party and – I can't breathe."

Lynda heard a sharp intake of breath through the phone.

This tightness in her chest had happened before, and it usually went away. But its persistence was the problem this time. And she knew that shortness of breath was a common symptom of a woman's heart attack.

"What's going on?" Mel asked.

"It feels like I'm breathing through a straw. And there's a burning in my chest, which I haven't felt before. I'm worried." Mel paced the Loft's tiny living area. He realized it was probably something minor, but Myrna's illness had also started with something seemingly insignificant. A slight pain, a shortness of breath. They'd thought it was nothing. He felt panic rising, but he kept his voice calm.

"Maybe you should go to the doctor," he suggested.

"I think that's a good idea. But it's Sunday, and my doctor's office is closed. Should I go to the emergency room or wait until tomorrow?" Lynda hung a right towards her house as they considered the options.

"You need to get checked out now. They'll clear you and on Tuesday, you'll be on your way to me."

"You think so? What if it's nothing?"

"It's best to err on the safe side. Trust me, I know. It's probably nothing, so why don't you let them tell you that? That way, you don't have to worry." Lynda agreed, changing route and heading towards the hospital. It was only seven at night.

She figured she'd probably be home by midnight.

CHAPTER FORTY
PANIC

Lynda dangled her feet over the edge of the examination table. A paper hospital gown draped her torso with its crude, stiff bulk. The doctor held a cold stethoscope on her back and instructed her to breathe deeply, something she found challenging. She'd spent two months in the hospital when she was very young, and almost died from pneumonia. Doctors and hospitals always provoked anxiety, but here, her anxiety was beginning to feel extreme. She wondered if it was interfering with her breathing. Maybe she was having a panic attack.

"I don't think it's my heart," she told the doctor, breathing. He moved to face her, stethoscope swinging from his neck. He was young and angular, with smooth, close-clipped hair. She doubted if he was thirty years old.

""You may be right, Ms. Saffell. But we should act as if it is until we find out exactly what's going on." He began flipping through her chart. "Your EKG came back normal, so perhaps this is some kind of spasm. I'll ordered a Lidocaine cocktail."

"Cocktail? " Lynda joked. "I can't believe my luck." The doctor chuckled, handing her chart to a nurse who was also young. She winked at Lynda.

"We call it that because it'll make you feel so good. You'll feel like it's girls' night out," the nurse told her.

"And, if it is a muscle spasm, you'll be able to breathe easier fairly quickly," the doctor added.

Both doctor and nurse were right. Within minutes, Lynda was breathing like a racehorse and feeling like she'd just downed a double martini. Her relief at knowing it was a spasm and not a heart attack was palpable, and she checked in with Mel as soon as she could. As she waited for discharge, she noticed her clothing laying limp and rumpled in a chair. She was wondering if she should start getting dressed when the nurse entered, followed by the doctor.

But instead of discharging her, he told her he needed more tests. She couldn't believe it.

"Why? If it's just a spasm?" she asked.

"Sometimes, spasms indicate stress in the esophagus caused by other conditions, like acid reflux. When there's too much acid in the wrong place, it debilitates the area, or even causes things like cancer." The sound of the word "cancer" squeezed Lynda's throat with fear. How did she go from spasm or panic attack to cancer?

"Cancer?"

"Don't worry, we don't think you have cancer. We just want to make sure there's no underlying problem. And we'll need you to stay overnight." Lynda's heart sank. She needed to pack and get on a plane to Vegas, not lay around for a bunch of precautionary tests. Still, she reasoned, it was better safe than sorry. "I've ordered an endoscopy first thing in the morning," he continued. "The nurse will fill you in."

As soon as they left, she called Mel. She wished the doctor hadn't used the word cancer. It was even worse than heart attack. She wanted to be told everything would be okay. That she would be okay. She calmed down after talking to him for a few minutes. Then, he brought up their trip.

"I guess we don't know if you'll be able to fly on Tuesday," he said. She could hear the disappointment in his voice. It mirrored her own.

"If I have anything to do with it, I'll be on that plane."

"Listen, Lynda, I just want you to be okay. Whatever it takes. Do I need to get on a plane and come to you?" He cleared his throat, silently reminding himself that what happened to Myrna was not happening to Lynda. To him. He tried to speak through a rising sense of dread. "Because I will. You know I will."

"No, I'm okay." She didn't want him to worry. "I'll be alright." She tried to sound confident. They remained silent for a few moments. Lynda heard the passing sounds of nurses and equipment outside the door.

"Lynda, if –" His voice cracked, his words evaporating before they formed. The thought of losing her like he'd lost Myrna was too much to bear. They'd had so little time together. He couldn't imagine life would actually be that cruel.

Lynda stared at the scuffed-up, dingy floor tiles, a harsh fluorescent light flickering overhead. She heard the distress in his voice and realized that he'd been through this before. That the word *cancer* struck him with more fear than she could possibly imagine. She steadied herself.

"Everything's going to be alright," she reassured him. "I'll get a clean bill of health tomorrow and be on my way."

The next day, Lynda's nurse rolled her into her hospital room to find her father sitting in a chair beside the bed. Even through the daze of medications and anesthetics, she could see he was worried. The last time she'd seen him, she'd told him about Mel and their trip to Vegas.

He'd been worried then, too.

He'd seen her go through mismatch and divorce. He'd wondered if it was too soon after Wade. And he knew Mel was a recent widower. His words came back to her. "Be careful, be careful with your heart." It was a lesson he'd learned from his marriage to her mother.

They talked quietly, her reassuring him, him bringing her cups of ice water she didn't really want but needed. Her dad knew about her Vegas plans, and though he might still have reservations, he didn't mention them. He only talked pleasantly about her trip, as if he had full faith she'd make it, and it would be good for her to relax.

Her spunky nurse, whose name she'd learned was Sharon, blew in and out on her rounds. And eventually, the doctor told her the endoscopy was clear, that they found nothing of concern. But before she could feel too relieved, he informed her that he wanted to do a quick ultrasound of her abdomen before discharging her, which he expected to do that afternoon.

This meant she'd make her plane, free and clear. Flushed with optimism, she called Mel, and left a cheery voice message. All her anxiety had dispersed, and she drifted off into peaceful slumber.

She was lucid and chatty as the technician globbed cold gel on her belly and began passing a large, black wand across her skin like a searchlight. She watched her shadowed insides ripple on the screen and looked forward to going home.

After a few minutes, the technician excused himself and returned with the doctor, whose vigilant expression aged his face as he examined the screen. The two talked quietly using indecipherable medical terminology. Then the doctor asked, "Do you see this, Ms. Saffell?" His tone was grave as he pointed to what looked like a tiny whirlpool on the screen.

"Yes," she answered hesitantly.

"It's a blood clot. It can be serious." He peered into the screen. "It's unusual in a healthy woman of your age, but we want to dissolve it. If it dislodges, it can cause swelling or internal bleeding. It could even be fatal." Before she could respond, he continued. "We need to put you on a blood thinner immediately, and you'll have to stay in the hospital until the clot dissipates, which could take a few days. Is there anyone you need to call?"

Fifteen minutes later, she stood despondently at the end of the hospital corridor holding a phone to her ear and trying to think clearly through her shock.

"This is not to be taken lightly," Mel said, distress edging his voice.

"I know. I don't think I'll be on that plane tomorrow." Her heart sank as she watched a breeze whipping palm trees outside a large window. She felt powerless....trapped.

"Lynda, if ..." It was the same sentence from the day before, only more despairing. She waited for him to finish. "I can't lose you, MP1. I can't lose you, too."

The next morning, Sharon plunged a needle into a bottle of blood thinner and sucked it up into a syringe as Lynda listened to Mel's voice, which had transformed to firm and determined overnight. The shades were still drawn and Lynda's voice echoed faintly in the dim room as she told Mel about calling the airline and informing them of her hospitalization. They'd put her on a flight to Vegas the following day, but she had no idea if she'd be discharged by then.

"We're putting too much energy into fear and worry over things that haven't happened yet," he said. Lynda thought about it. She stared at her half-eaten breakfast of wilted, mealy pancakes and tin-flavored applesauce.

"Yes, you're right, but I really want to be on that plane tomorrow."

"Good, we're going to manifest this. If you get on that plane, that means you're well. How are we going to make sure you get on the plane?"

"I don't know. I'm afraid I'll be lying around here all day while the clot dissolves. And you know how it is. I'm going to be on their schedule. They could care less if I have a plane to catch tomorrow."

"Not necessarily."

"What do you mean?"

"Do you remember the story about eagles vs. ducks?"

"Eagles vs. ducks?" She was puzzled. Then she remembered. He'd talked about eagles and ducks sometimes in the course room. Ducks blindly follow rules. Eagles make things happen.

"Lynda, let's imagine your eagle is there, and he or she can help you. Is waiting to help you. All you have to do is find that person." Lynda bit her lip, mentally scrolling through the staff she'd met so far. In her mind, they had pasty faces and weary voices. They were definitely ducks.

As she contemplated this, Sharon raised the blinds with a crisp movement, flooding the room with light. She put her hand on her hip, a satisfied smile on her face.

"That's better. It's a beautiful, sunny day outside," she said to Lynda.

"Mel," Lynda said into the phone as she stared at Sharon. "I think I just found my eagle."

Throughout the day, Mel and Lynda practiced visualizing her getting her discharge papers and checking her suitcase, asking a stewardess for some water, shading her eyes from Vegas's scorching sun. And as soon as she got the chance, Lynda pulled Sharon aside and explained her situation.

"The airline said there's a seat for me on a plane tomorrow, but it's the only one." Sharon nodded, assuming an empathetic, slightly vague expression on her face. "The thing is, I'm meeting my new boyfriend." At this, Sharon pulled up a chair. "We've had this beautiful, amazing thing for two months, but we've only seen each other a few days out of that time. This trip was our first chance to spend time together without distractions. If I don't make the plane tomorrow, it won't happen."

"What?" Sharon demanded, as if protesting an injustice. Lynda knew her eagle was in flight.

"Sharon, what needs to happen so I can get out of here and be on that plane?" Sharon looked thoughtful.

"Well, the blood clot needs to dissolve."

"Is that it?"

"Mmm-hmm. And your ultrasound isn't scheduled yet." Lynda looked at her hopefully. "But, it's been a day so it could already be dissolved, I suppose."

"Well, when is the earliest I can get that ultrasound?" The question ignited a new, fiercer look on Sharon's face.

"I don't know," she said. She was positively resolute. "But I'm going to find out 'cause tomorrow you are going to Vegas to see your man!"

By noon the next day, Sharon twirled into Lynda's room proudly brandishing discharge papers high in the air. "We did it, girlfriend!" she exclaimed triumphantly. "You're out of here, free and clear!" They squealed with excitement, causing curious passersby to glance into the room. Then, Lynda jumped up and looked at her watch.

"Oh, my God!" she exclaimed. "I only have two hours to go home, pack, and get to the airport!"

CHAPTER FORTY-ONE
WELCOME TO MY WORLD, MP1

The lever of the dollar slot machine felt sticky as Mel pulled it towards him and watched the reel spin. But he didn't care if any of the large, garish symbols lined up. He just wanted to see Lynda. He'd been waiting in the Las Vegas airport for an hour, checking the arrival screen relentlessly. He checked his watch, his brow furrowing with concern as he noted that her plane was late. Then three cartoonish cherries lined up, and the machine's big, red siren began flashing. A woman with gray hair bound in a grubby golf hat grinned at him from the next machine. She was missing two teeth. He watched his machine spit gold coins into its tray, trying to count them as they poured out.

"Eighty bucks," he muttered through a half-hearted surge of adrenaline. Then, he collected, went to baggage claim, and found it bleak and empty. He fished out his phone to see if she would pick up.

"Where are you?" he heard Lynda ask on the other end.

"I'm at baggage claim waiting for you. Where are you?" To his great confusion and surprise, she said she was actually outside looking for him. He swiveled his head towards the sliding glass doors the led outside and scanned for her.

"I don't know what happened but your flight didn't show up on the monitor," he explained as he stepped outside and saw her standing on the sidewalk, her body turned away from him so she couldn't see him. "But I'm here now. Turn around."

Relief washed through him as she turned to look at him. He knew he'd been shaken by her health scare, but seeing her now, he suddenly realized it had reopened the wound left by love and loss. This wound rooted itself in a primal part of him where his deepest fears slept, a part that recognized only one reality, whether someone was *here* or *not here*.

Until he saw her walking towards him, beautiful, healthy and very much *here*, that part of him was finally reassured. He took her in his arms in a cacophony of feelings, the blinding sting of grateful tears in his eyes. Something within him knew he'd never let her go.

"The good news is you're here," he managed to say through his emotion, "And," he added more matter-of-factly, "I won eighty bucks to take you to dinner." Lynda beamed, but she also looked thinner and more pale than usual as she blinked into Nevada's mid-afternoon sun. They quickly decided to head to the Loft, settle in, and have an early meal. The Loft was parked at Sam's Town, a kitschy, Vegas-style resort that catered to RV'ers. It was off-season, so he'd obtained one of the prime sites.

"I got us a good spot. Right by the hotel," Mel exclaimed as he pulled up beside the Loft and got out. This would be her first time staying in the Loft, and he wanted everything to be perfect. As she got out of the car, he pointed to the towering resort, telling her excitedly about the carpeted casino, movie theater, steakhouse, and live shows waiting within. Then he grabbed her bags and followed her to the door. A piece of notebook paper with big, black letters scrawled on it was taped to the door, corners flapping in the dusty breeze. He watched her as she leaned in, squinting, to read it.

"MP1," she read, knowing it was his abbreviation for 'My Precious One.' "Welcome to My World."

Vegas melted the trouble and turmoil of the past few days as if it never happened, and they fell into an easy routine. In the mornings, they hiked or swam. Afternoons found them napping and grazing at the resort's cantina. And at night, they drifted along the Strip's electric river.

They kissed and talked, ducking in and out of glitzy casinos, lively cafes, and glamorous hotel lobbies. They attended shows, and when they were over, shuffled past street vendors costumed as golden showgirls. They beheld fountains splashing in moonlight, posed in front of iconic marquees, and trekked the length of the city's buzzing glow. The crowds, though thinner than at high-season, were still formidable, and Mel held Lynda's hand as they weaved in and out of loud, chaotic lines.

For months, they'd been kept apart by distance and work. Over that time, it was the few days they *had* spent together, along with their nightly phone conversations, that had eased the falling away of their old friendship. In its place was something much deeper, and in Vegas, they were finally able to cement that new bond, delighting in the sheer adventure of learning about one another.

One night, they found themselves in the Coyote Ugly souvenir shop, laughing as they navigated tight displays of shot glasses, sunblock, key chains, t-shirts, and racy underwear. Lynda snatched a pair of black panties from a rack and half-jokingly held them to her waist.

"Try 'em on," he suggested, dangling them in the air. As if seeing his bid and raising him, Lynda grinned, plucking the silky fabric from the hanger, and tossing it on the ground. Confused, he stared down at it nearly touching the toes of his leather sandals.

"The best way to try panties on is to throw them on the floor and see how they look," Lynda explained. Mel looked up at her, poised for the punchline. He'd come to cherish her spontaneity, and it pleased him that he never quite knew what to expect. "'Cause that's where they'll be most of the time!"

Buoyant and laughing, she picked them off the floor and carried them to the cashier.

"Ring these up. We're going home," Mel boasted to the cashier from behind her. "Wait – hold on," he added, plunking a bottle of red wine down beside the underwear. "We'll take this, too." He recalled how nervous he'd been at her house for their first date, and was amazed at how much his anxiety had shifted in a few short weeks.

Before, her raw sexuality and free spirit had attracted him and simultaneously intimidated him. Forty-plus years of marriage made him comfortable with intimacy and romance with Myrna, but he'd been at a complete loss about how to date or be intimate with someone else. He realized now that anyone would've felt that way, that it had been a crisis of familiarity and habit, one that in time, when he wasn't looking, would be replaced with a dazzling, effortless comfort. Though he hadn't expected their time in Vegas to be difficult or awkward, he was overjoyed with their first burst of uninterrupted time, as if it had always, and would always, belong to them.

When they arrived at the Loft later, they drank the wine and settled into a playful evening of caresses and relaxed banter. The crumpled, white plastic bag holding the panties sat forgotten on the couch. But as the clock edged towards midnight, the wine made them drowsy, something Mel commented on with regret.

"I hate to say this but I'm really sleepy," he told her. Lynda reclined fully into the back of the couch and reached for his hand. Then she yawned.

"Me, too," she said simply. "Wanna call it a night?" Mel paused. Sleep was all he wanted to do, but how would she perceive it? A tiny part him feared being inadequate.

"I wanted for us to be together," He tried not to let his obvious disappointment show. "But, I'm too exhausted for love tonight."

"It's okay if we just cuddle." He looked over at her, trying to discern if her words were as genuine as they sounded. She didn't seem fazed at all.

She took his hand in hers, then lifted their clasped hands in front of them as if holding up an example.

"I like all of it," she said. "Touching, being close. Intimacy isn't always about sex or achieving a goal." She kissed his hand and gazed at him dreamily. "It's about this, too."

"Really?" he asked, regarding her. He'd always defined sex rather narrowly, and believed that it, and it alone, expressed intimacy. Her more expansive ideas opened him up to new possibilities and reassured him.

Lynda nodded, letting their clasped hands arc back to the couch like a fallen star. "Let's go to bed."

He smiled, stood up, and began leading her back to the Loft's cozy bedroom. Then he turned around, glancing at the panty bag on the couch. "We forgot your panties," he joked.

Lynda winked. "No matter. We can put them where they belong tomorrow."

Several hours later, they awoke from a deep, dreamless sleep. Mel heard Lynda ask through the darkness if he was awake. He looked at the clock. It was three-thirty. Neither of them had any idea why they'd woken up, but after talking for ten minutes, they knew they weren't going back to sleep anytime soon. She sat up and turned the bedside lamp on.

The night took on the mischievous, energized air of a sleepover as they took turns suggesting things to do, giggling like a couple of preteen girls. Then Mel remembered the pile of DVDs in the cupboard.

"Wanna watch Larry the Cable Guy?" he asked. Lynda tossed her head back and laughed.

"Yes!" she answered with satisfaction. "Yes, I do want to watch Larry the Cable Guy."

It turned out to be some of the best entertainment of the week.

Hi LYNNEY, MP I
WELCOME
To MY
WORLD

Lynda found this on the door of the RV in Las Vegas, NV

Mel & Lynda on the Vegas Strip

CHAPTER FORTY-TWO
GARDEN OF HUMMINGBIRDS

It was one hundred and five degrees on their last day in Vegas, and they'd escaped the heat and driven west to Mt. Charleston, hovering seven thousand five hundred refreshing feet above the desert town. Leaving Mel's car at the Lodge, they began their climb in the cooler temperatures towards Cathedral Rock, a landmark that opened to views of Kyle Canyon several hundred feet below.

Lynda trailed slightly behind Mel as she negotiated the dusty switchbacks, which grew steeper as they neared the peak. She listened to the rhythm of their breathing become more strained, and watched hawks wheeling overhead out of the corner of her eye. She couldn't help but notice Mel's tanned calves flex as he climbed. It was hard for her to believe she'd been concerned about their eighteen-year age difference. He was more vital and fit than most people her age, and he seemed more youthful than ever.

When she'd arrived in Vegas, she knew they shared a profound attraction. She was eager to learn more about it, and she knew she'd have fun doing so. But the trip had shown her that their compatibility reached far beyond her expectations. It felt more like she was on a honeymoon than a trip with a boyfriend.

As they climbed, she thought about their previous evening. They'd been eating dinner, talking cozily. Sometime around dessert, the subject meandered to Couples 101, an RYL course Mel hadn't offered for the past two years. She'd experienced the course as a student couple with Wade, and later, they'd volunteered as an assistant couple. In the Couple's Course, Mel and Myrna had inspired her with their instruction. She'd never seriously thought about being a facilitator for couples, because most of her time in RYL had been focused on learning to love herself, and she'd only recently grokked that she deserved to have an equal partner in love. That's why she felt so honored and surprised when Mel asked her what she thought about teaching a course for couples with him.

"I'd love to," she'd exclaimed, plunging a spoon into a slice of cheesecake, enjoying its spongy sweetness. "It would be an honor." But as she said this, she wondered if she had what it takes. Though she had participated in countless RYL courses, as well as several Couples weekends, she'd never sat in the instructor's seat. And Mel had only instructed with Myrna. If she became his Couples teaching partner, what would that imply about their relationship?

As they talked more about it, she reasoned that her experience as wife, single mom, and long-term girlfriend would accommodate a broad range of experiences and dynamics in relationships. What she didn't say was that nurturing a loving relationship with a life partner, a soul mate even, felt like her life's path or purpose.

She didn't know *why* having a life partner, or even being a good partner, felt so important to her. It had just always been that way. Of course, she had other aspirations, and she no longer *needed* a relationship to validate or complete her. But throughout her adult life, she'd existed in a field of romantic expectation and hope. Now, maybe she'd get the opportunity to not only live that vision but share it as a teacher.

As they talked more about the exciting possibilities, their relationship shifted to a deeper, richer level. The last vestiges of Mel as a friend and mentor of six years evaporated. Now, he sat before her, not only as an equal partner, but as a peer. His invitation was evidence that he was regarding her that way, too. She felt that she was finally stepping into her potential, and what she had held hope for was becoming a reality. The luster of that new reality still clung to her as she crested Cathedral Rock and took in the light-drenched vista of the Spring Mountains unfolding in both directions. She'd just taken her place beside Mel and shaded her eyes against the sun when she noticed something that felt like a tiny miracle.

"Mel, look there!" She pointed at a couple sitting across the expanse dangling their legs over the edge of the rock. It was like seeing a reflection of themselves. An expression of wonder overcame Mel's face as he regarded them, obviously feeling what she felt. "They look so much like us, we could take their picture and say it was us." Mel took out his camera and handed it to her.

"What do you think it means?" he asked. "That we're in the right place?" Lynda smiled and shrugged.

"Maybe it means we're in the right love," she offered simply, knowing that he'd know exactly what she meant.

Forty-five minutes later, they sat back at the lodge admiring its twenty-foot cathedral ceiling. Kyle Canyon added to the drama served as a backdrop to the lodge with its forbidding rock wall. Enormous windows lined three sides of the room, framing Mt. Charleston's fir, aspen, and ponderosa forests. The spectacular view was only outmatched by dozens of hummingbirds swooping so near to the windows that Lynda imagined herself reaching out to touch them. The restaurant was mostly empty.

They ordered drinks at the bar and settled in. Mel mentioned that he'd be driving to California to visit friends after she flew back to Florida. He'd been so excited about connecting with kindred spirits and looked forward to walking on San Clemente Beach when he'd made his original plan to drive cross country, culminating in Orange County, California. Airplane tickets were already purchased for his flights to Tampa and back out of John Wayne Airport for the September RYL course. But things were different now, and he questioned his intentions.

Why am I going to California? His relationship with Lynda had progressed to a whole new level the past week. He knew they'd be together again in another ten days, but after that... how much longer?

"I know you have to get back to work and the kids, but I wish you could join me on the road. It's been such a wonderful time here together, and I don't want it to end." Mel reached out and took her hand.

"I feel the same way. I will miss you, but you'll be back for the course soon." Lynda swirled her drink with the straw, deep in thought. "When do you plan to drive the motorhome back home?" She was almost afraid to hear his answer. She couldn't bear the thought of only seeing him once a month when he returned to teach RYL.

"Well, my plan was to stay about a month on the west coast, but now I have more incentive to get back home than I do to stay in California." Relieved, Lynda squeezed his hand and smiled.

Even though they both felt sadness at the prospect of parting, they did their best to relive their favorite moments from the trip. "I can't wait to get our pictures developed. Especially those of the tigers at the Mirage and of our hike today!"

Mel grew silent and sipped his water. Lynda knew he had a taciturn side, but she could also sense the shift in his energy. He seemed faraway suddenly as he stared out the window. A hummingbird pecked at the glass as it zipped by, interrupting his reverie. He reassured her as he explained.

"I just remembered Myrna's picture tucked away in a drawer back in the Loft. I was thinking about how I don't want to look at it." Lynda covered his hand with hers. She stayed quiet and waited. "Or even think about. I took it when she was sick, only weeks before she died. I . . ." Here he trailed off and watched the birds. "It's not how I want to remember her."

Lynda could hear the anguish he'd lived through. As she thought about the picture, she joined him in watching the windows swarming with birds. The waiter had told them that aside from several species of hummingbirds, there were chickadees, goldfinches, and violet-throated swallows. "We feed them twice a day," he'd said. She understood why Mel didn't want to look at the picture, but she knew it wasn't good to actively avoid it either. She'd heard him say so many times, *what we resist persists*.

"Maybe you should try to look at it again," she offered simply. He agreed, then asked if she wanted to see the picture. She draped her arm around his upper back and laid her head on his shoulder as if her entire body replied back to him, *anything, of course*. "Maybe there's a message there. Something that will offer you more clarity." As she spoke, she could feel an actual change in her body. It was a sensation that didn't erase any despair or darkness from her past but instead unfurled it into a brighter fullness, one petal at a time, like a flower.

Abandon and joy surged within her as memories of her time in Las Vegas swirled like the birds outside, leaving her with the heady impression of having finally found something long desired and searched for. She watched a tender, blue-breasted bird squabble for a place at the feeder and win, its eye glinting iridescent in the sun.

Mel and Lynda on hike to Cathedral Rock

CHAPTER FORTY-THREE
THE TORCH

Lynda tossed an open business envelope on the kitchen counter, unfolded another official-looking letter, and began to read. A dwindling stack of junk mail and a cup of fresh coffee lay within reach. She glanced at the pile, feeling slightly disappointed. She thought she'd already sorted through all the mail, but somehow she'd missed some. She checked the time, opened the blinds, and squinted at Tampa's mid-morning sun as it cascaded through the window. It was cleaning day. She'd been home for a week.

Once she finished the mail, she carried a dusting cloth and bottle of cleaner into the living room, where she knelt in front of the TV console and turned on her favorite Karla Bonoff album. She sang along enthusiastically as she swept the cloth over the console's surfaces, enjoying the repetition of it. When the simple, plaintive notes of a piano began to play, half-recognizing the song, she turned the volume up until it filled the room.

Oh, we never know where life will take us. We know it's just a ride on the wheel.

The lyrics seemed to conjure up the name of the song, *Goodbye My Friend*. Something about it struck her, and immediately she thought of Myrna. She continued dusting, allowing the music to pull her emotional focus towards it, sharpening and narrowing it. The lyrics, which were sad, began to reverberate deeper, and Lynda began to feel herself overcome with emotion.

And we never know when death will shake us, and we wonder how it will feel . . .

A humble, quiet desire to pause came over her, as if she'd asked a question and waited for an answer. Her hands stopped moving as she sat back on her heels with the vague awareness that she was taking a common yoga position she often taught her students.

Hero pose, it was called.

The sunbeams created geometric shapes on the floor beside her, appearing ghostly and unreal. Above them, dust particles swirled, suspending themselves mid-air. As the lyrics crystallized in her mind, she began to feel the gnawing of loss and sadness fill her heart. Myrna's face was so clear in Lynda's mind that, in an instant, it seemed to trigger all the moments she'd spent with her friend, leaving the ache of grief behind. Lynda's body tilted towards the music, wholly attentive. She'd continued singing along, but now felt her voice tighten as it slowly faded away like an unfinished sentence.

So, goodbye my friend, I know I'll never see you again but the time together through all these years will take away these tears.

As she felt tears prick her eyes, a warmth, as if from a blanket being wrapped around her, crept down her back, simultaneously flowing around her shoulders. This ethereal hug seemed to reassure her, as a sense of loving compassion swept over her.

I'm okay now, she heard herself sing along again, her voice tender as the mental image of Myrna's face transformed into the warm presence she felt now, one that seemed to sing with her. Through her.

And as it did, she realized the song's bold truth: it actually was okay.

She didn't know how she knew, but she was suddenly certain that Myrna was with her, and they were both okay. Perhaps there was still reason to feel sad, but sitting here, there was more reason to feel comfort. Or, comforted. And as she opened her eyes to a mystical world where Myrna's spirit was somehow helping her move through her sadness, she did.

She felt touched, and longed for the connection to continue, as when loved ones who've died visit in the sweetness of dreams. She blinked, the walls still in shadow. Grids of sunlight dragged themselves imperceptibly across the floor. And as the song concluded, she heard something else, something that wasn't her mind or the song but that reached through her and spoke.

I'm passing you the torch, it said, in a clear, inner voice that sounded like hers but wasn't. She covered her mouth and stared down, listening to hear more.

The presence faded and was gone.

"Did she say anything else?" Mel asked later over the phone. Lynda reclined in bed, a half-finished crossword puzzle on the nightstand. She'd just told him about her afternoon experience.

"No, that's all I heard. *I'm passing you the torch.* And then she was gone." They paused, both in thought. Then Mel broke the silence.

"What do you think it means?"

"That I'm crazy?" Lynda said, half-incredulous. Mel didn't laugh.

"It must mean something. I'm thinking back to when I was at Melanie's house taking care of Joshie and the phone rang –."

"– but neither of us actually called the other."

"Exactly. And do you remember when I said, 'someone must want us to talk'? It could've been a glitch, but then again...could it have been Myrna? And what happened to you today...I've learned to trust your intuition or sixth sense, whatever it is." Lynda pondered this. She believed in life after death, but she'd never had an experience that tested that belief until now. In the moment, she felt certain it was Myrna's presence she felt, but now she was second-guessing herself. And knowing some people wouldn't believe it was possible, she was grateful she was able to share it with Mel.

"When it was happening, I felt dazed but clear at the same time. It was like she was telling me something, and I was trying to listen."

"What do you think she was trying to tell you?"

"Something besides passing the torch. She didn't want me to be sad about losing her. She wanted to reassure me, to know she was okay. And she was comforting me. Telling me I was okay, too."

"But what does that have to do with passing a torch?" Not wanting to overthink her answer, Lynda closed her eyes and tried to tap into the visceral knowing that had gripped her earlier. She wanted to trust herself and her experience.

"I felt so connected to her, like she was right there in the room embracing me. And giving me a message. She wanted me to know that I would take care of you now."

"I don't exactly need taking care of. I'm doing a pretty good job on my own."

"I know, but it's like she grounded you. And now it's my turn to do that. It's what she wants." They each thought about this, Lynda lying in her bed and Mel sitting on his guest bed for the night, an uncomfortable fold-out sofa in a friend's dim living room. A floor lamp spilled light on the floor. He thought of Myrna's picture back at the Loft. He didn't know what any of it meant, but he felt like he was beginning to. He'd always felt Myrna grounded him. Maybe she thought he needed someone else to ground him now. Maybe, wherever she was, she still wanted him to be happy.

"I just thought about her picture, why she wanted me to take it." He hesitated, changing course. "I still don't know – maybe she wants us to know she's watching over us, that she's still involved somehow."

"Have you looked at it yet?" Lynda asked. Mel was quiet. He hadn't thought much about it since Las Vegas.

"Is that what she might want?" he asked, more to himself than anyone else.

"Things are changing," she said, patting down the bedspread in smooth strokes, as if soothing a cat. Then she yawned and looked at the clock. It was almost midnight. She didn't know if Myrna wanted Mel to look at the picture, but it was possible it held a message of some kind, especially in light of her afternoon.

He asked if she was tired, and she pulled the bedspread up, suddenly overtaken by drowsiness. "Yes, I am." She knew the routine. Mel would put her to bed, reciting a prayer he said every evening for her. It made her feel safe, loved, and protected. She knew it by heart but never tired of hearing him say it.

"Today is over," he started. "I did the best I could. I'm grateful for today, and now it's time to rest my body and my mind." Lynda rolled over, clicked the light off and lay on her side, staring into the darkness. A faint clap of thunder sounded in the distance. "I invite my angels into my dreams to teach me while I'm asleep. And when I wake up in the morning, I'll remember everything my angels have taught me." She believed in angels. And she knew he did, too. She closed her eyes and waited for the final line. "And when I wake up in the morning, I'll be alive, alert, and feeling great."

CHAPTER FORTY-FOUR
WHILE I SLEEP

The next day, Mel pulled his hands from his pockets, shaded his eyes, and watched the surfers twist their boards up and down the breakers several yards out. Their bodies tumbled silently into the ocean, bobbing into view a few seconds later. Sometimes, they undulated along a wave's writhing spine like snakes in a midnight garden. It looked both peaceful and difficult, an obsessive process of wrangling turbulence into tranquility. He tucked his hand back in his pockets and continued walking the picturesque shore at San Clemente's famous pier.

He thought about his conversation with Lynda the night before. He still hadn't looked at Myrna's picture yet, as Lynda had suggested. He was still kicking around all the possible meanings of *passing the torch.*

The torch could refer to some kind of responsibility or action. It could also be a symbol of some kind. An idea or philosophy. It was when someone allowed someone else to do the work they were doing, or support the ideas they supported. If Lynda was correct, Myrna was communicating that she was passing on the role of grounding him. Or, was she passing along the actual role of partner?

One thing was for sure. Since Myrna's funeral, he'd harbored suspicions that she could be reaching out. Not only to him, but to others. But he also was intentional to check in with his inner guidance. He realized that, as a new widower, he might be subconsciously looking for a way to comfort himself. But if that were the case, why would he hear all these stories, and from completely different sources? He closed his eyes, quieting his breathing, and allowed the question to resonate within him.

Now, his suspicions were confirmed. Myrna, or her spirit, was making her presence known.

But why?

Mel's cell phone startled him mid-thought. He looked at the caller ID and answered. It was Cindy. He was flying to Tampa in a few days to teach, so she was probably checking in. He found a dry patch of sand and sat down.

"Mel, I'm so glad I caught you!" he heard her exclaim over the line.

"Hello, yourself!" he replied. He was genuinely happy to hear from her. They chatted for a few minutes, she commenting how beautiful she'd heard California was, he remarking that he was looking for dolphins as they spoke. Then she asked how long he'd been gone, and if he had plans to come home soon. He wasn't sure how to answer.

He considered his nomadic existence.

First, the Loft had been his and Myrna's home. Now it was his. His townhouse in Indian Shores was rented out to Carol. Then he thought of Lynda.

"Well, I plan to be home for the winter. I have a reservation at the RV park in Seminole, and then, who knows?" He knew his heart was with Lynda, yet he still felt the thrill of not needing to know the details. *Surrender and trust the process* was a motto he lived by.

"So what are your plans when you fly in this month?" Cindy inquired, curious if she would need to pick him up when he arrived.

"I'll be flying in on Wednesday, as usual. Lynda is picking me up from the airport, and I'm staying with her for the weekend." Mel watched a gull peck at the sand, and size him up for handouts. As usual for gulls, it seemed aggressive. He ignored it.

"Well, do you want to stay here?" Cindy asked.

"No, thank you. I'll be staying with Lynda," he answered.

"What about staying one night at my place?" Cindy continued.

Mel felt himself grow tense and uncomfortable with Cindy's question. Hadn't she just asked him this? Why was she asking again? "No. I'll be staying with Lynda." he repeated, trying to keep the edge out of his voice.

"Well, okay, if that's what you want." She sounded disappointed, and he struggled to understand why she was asking him at all. She knew that he and Lynda were in a relationship. Mel felt awkward, and he wondered, *what was her motive?*

By the time they got off the phone, such thoughts had pushed all thoughts of the torch out of his mind. But he hadn't forgotten about Myrna's picture.

He studied the same gull, still strutting around territorial, sullen, and empty-mouthed. Then he made the kind of unanticipated decision that people often make when they say something very innocent, only to realize later that as they did so, an important threshold had already been crossed.

"Gotta go," he said to the gull confidently. "I have a date with a picture." The gull leveled a blank stare and flew away.

He took it slowly when he got back to the Loft. He ate a nicer dinner than usual, drank some wine, called Lynda. Then he took a hot shower. When it was time to go to bed, he reached for the photo envelope and pulled Myrna's picture out. He stared down at it for a very long time.

At first, the familiar pain rushed up, the instinct to scan, to avoid. But he forced himself to look at it, into it. He beheld it.

And from the cavern of her last days, Myrna stared back.

Memories of her illness, of losing her so fast and not being able to do a thing about it, rushed back. The sense of helplessness and loss that had overridden everything *then* had been horrible, but ultimately, they weren't the total cause of his apprehension now.

Now, he realized that despite losing what *seemed* like everything at the time, after all of it was gone, something lingered. There was still something precious to lose. Otherwise, he wouldn't avoid looking at the picture. What was it?

He closed his eyes and let the image from the picture sink in. He waited for some kind of answer to his question, some reason, but none came. After a while, he opened his eyes, looked at the image once more, and put the picture away.

As he settled into bed, her image floated up in his mind's eye. But it wasn't the one from the picture. She appeared as he always remembered her, vibrant and strong. As he considered this image, he suddenly realized that his avoidance wasn't about not wanting to face something. It was about fearing that the image in the picture would somehow erase or replace the memory of her that lived inside of him.

Now, he was certain it never would, no matter how long he stared at her last photograph. For him, she'd exist in his heart as he'd always known her, beautifully, as she'd lived her life.

A few moments later, his nightly prayer tasted sweeter as he spoke it in the darkness, for no one but himself.

Today is over. I did the best I could. I'm grateful for today to rest my body and my mind. I invite my angels to teach me while I'm asleep and when I wake up, I'll remember everything . . .

It was later that night, in time out of time, that a dawnless light rose.

In a wakeful sleep, a dreamless dream, he watched Myrna's face crystallize. In an instant, it was absolutely clear. It was the same face he'd contemplated earlier, the one she wore when she was younger and full of life. Her dark hair fell richly to her shoulders and appeared backlit, as if she stood in front of strong sunlight, but he couldn't see the source of the light.

She smiled.

Words formed in his mind without effort or thought, as if he'd long ago planned exactly what to say when they next met. The words were like transmissions, immediate, lucid, and precise. Except he hadn't planned anything. They formed three questions and originated from one thing only – an inarticulate, oceanic longing he carried.

The first question. *Why did you want me to take your picture?*

Her mouth didn't move, yet he heard her reply. *I wanted you to take my picture so that when you looked at it, you'd see how much pain I was in and you wouldn't be angry with me for asking to leave.*

Her answer recalled the last words she'd ever spoke to him, as clearly as if she'd spoke them yesterday. As if she were speaking them now.

These words were no vision, dream, or visitation. In his mind, he became who he was when she spoke them. He cradled her head, held a cup of water to her lips. Her effort to drink moved thick in his bones. She looked up at him, voice weak, eyes weepy, and said, "I want to go home." He could still hear it, still see her lips and throat move as she spoke, still see the shadow of their bodies joining on the wall.

The memory blurred and slipped away, and his second question formed. *Did you have anything to do with. . .*

He was unable to complete his question about him and Lynda before, from somewhere beyond her smile, beyond both of them, she simply said *yes.*

He barely had time to consider her answer before he felt her begin to turn, the shadows on her face growing long, dark, and deep. He knew the next question would be his last.

It was one he never expected he'd have the opportunity to ask. *But for what purpose?*

He needed to know why she was putting all this energy into communicating, and into bringing love into his life. Her face, still smiling, swam closer even as it receded. She bestowed her final answer.

You'll see.

As he heard these words, he blinked his eyes open and discovered it was morning.

She was beyond him.

CHAPTER FORTY-FIVE
THE LAST DRIVE

As he mulled over the past few months, Mel wondered. Had he been running away from something or toward it?

Sometimes in life, it was hard to tell.

So, he drank his beer impassively, watched a football game on TV, and thought about it all. He was sitting in a Dallas restaurant for what felt like his thousandth restaurant meal. The place featured thick steaks, Gulf oysters, smoky barbecue, beer, and typical Texas swagger. Food this good should never feel routine, but there it was. Still, there was one thing that was different. It was his birthday, and he and the Loft were en route to Tampa.

It was the last leg of the road trip.

Over the past few weeks, he and Lynda had talked at length about Myrna's visits, and what they could mean. They puzzled over her enigmatic last answer, *you'll see*, but never reached any satisfactory conclusions.

Why would Myrna play matchmaker from beyond? What could she possibly want? He still didn't know for sure. How could he?

He thought of Myrna's funeral, how the procession formed a caravan to the horizon. He thought about leaving Tampa and heading for New Orleans. It felt like so long ago, even though it had only been four months. He'd driven north, tears streaming down his cheeks, nothing but the sound of windshield wipers swiping at the falling rain.

He remembered how surreal it was to be so alone, then how freeing. He thought about winding up and down craggy mountain trails, going exactly where he wanted to go, when he wanted to. He remembered creating his Ideal Partner list, the deep pang of grief the first time he saw Myrna's last picture, feeling fireworks thunder through his bones as he held Lynda's hand on the beach. He thought of how both his and Lynda's Ideal Partner lists matched almost perfectly. And he remembered wandering Las Vegas with her, how their laughter came from nowhere and their intimacy deepened. All the phone calls by moonlight, all the milky stars rising over canyons in silhouette.

The uncanny shape of things falling into place. The little miracles.

He reviewed the evidence of Myrna's continued presence. The first signs were tiny things that happened to other people, like when his friend walked into a Colorado hotel the day of Myrna's funeral and saw the staff wearing Hawaiian shirts in winter. The mysterious phone call between him and Lynda. What, or who, had connected them that morning? Then Myrna, strong and direct, came to Lynda and comforted her. Then, Mel's vision.

You'll see.

As he recalled these words, he became aware of his body. His hand was uncomfortably cold. Then he noticed he was still holding his beer bottle. He took another swig, thought *Happy Birthday to Me* as he set it on the bar top, and glanced down at his empty plate. He didn't understand everything in life, didn't know the reason Myrna had connected him with Lynda, didn't even know if she'd known herself. But he didn't doubt that something otherworldly was happening. There was simply too much evidence.

And he had grown tired of restaurant food, and all the Amy's pizzas in the Loft. He was ready to go home now. To land somewhere to call home again.

If he'd been searching for something, running towards something, he'd found it. Or, maybe it had found him.

Myrna was his soul mate and that never ended. But as he thought of her involvement, he couldn't help but wonder if it was possible to have a second soul mate. He'd never heard anything about that. Could that be what she was trying to tell him?

How else could he have transitioned so quickly from losing her to finding Lynda?

When Lynda asked him to hasten his return back to Tampa, it was one of the easiest decisions he'd ever made.

She'd been expressing frustration with the miles between them for some time. At first, she'd encouraged and supported his travels, but as time went on, and especially after Las Vegas, she grew impatient with the distance. It was time for his solo, as she called it, to end. And as he paid his ticket and rose to leave, he couldn't agree more.

He would be home soon.

And as the restaurant's heavy wooden doors swung behind him, he thought that he liked the idea of home.

Now, it would be wherever Lynda was.

Mel arrived in Tallahassee within a day of leaving Texas. Since Brandy had just started her freshman year at Florida State, they organized a weekend reunion of sorts. Lynda would be riding up from Tampa with Nick, Brandy's long-distance sweetheart, so that the four could be together.

It tickled Mel to remember how Brandy and Nick sparked their romance in the same place that he and Lynda had. What were the odds? Then again, what were the odds of any of this happening?

The four drank rich coffee, ate meals, and strolled around Lake Ella watching flocks of geese and swans. Tallahassee was famous for its moss-draped live oaks. The trees, decades old, ringed the lake's perimeter, providing a magical canopy. They all laughed when two burly wind-worn pelicans broke the ranks, sending ducks spitting and squawking in every direction. The geese, accustomed to going unchallenged, scampered onto the grassy shore.

It all felt incredibly ordinary, and because of that, completely wonderful, as if a new life were beginning for all of them. After lunch on Sunday, Lynda and Mel climbed in the Loft together and headed home to Tampa.

Mel planned to pit-stop near Gainesville, midway between Tampa and Tallahassee, to take a break from driving. The ride to Gainesville was uneventful, except for the fact that Lynda's mom called, tipsy as usual but in an agreeable enough mood. That's what Lynda thought, at least, until her mom jokingly told her to put the "Jew-boy on the phone." Lynda feared her eyes might roll out of her head onto the Loft's floorboard. She'd never quite got used to her mom's TMI policies and crass sense of humor, and she wasn't sure Mel was ready for it either.

When Mel asked what her mom had said, she hoped it was because he wanted in on the joke. Still, she cringed at the thought of what her mother might say to him.

"She said she wants to talk to the Jew-boy," she told him. Not one to be intimidated, Mel smiled and took the phone. Like a sassy, Floridian May West, Lynda's mother led with her pleasant, albeit slightly shocking banter. She told him she hoped he wasn't offended by her sense of humor, but the amused tone in her voice also let him know she didn't give a damn if he was.

He knew the only way to win someone like her over was to show her he could handle any curve balls she threw his way, no matter how raunchy, unexpected, or off-color. And he could.

Besides, she was kind of funny.

"I don't see what there is to be offended about. There's nothing wrong with being a Jew-boy, after all," he quipped.

"You know, Mel, you're absolutely right." She paused to take a sip from her drink. "I just wanted you to know, I've never seen my daughter happier...and, I just wanted to thank you." He felt like he already knew her mom from everything Lynda had shared about her over the years. But candor? This he wasn't expecting. Feeling a sudden warmth spread over his face, he glanced at Lynda, who looked over at him anxiously. He rested a reassuring hand on her knee.

"That means a lot to me, Mama. Making your daughter as happy as she makes me is very important to me." As Lynda listened to him say this, her shoulders visibly relaxed and she smiled. And when she spoke again, Mel heard Lynda's mom's voice soften.

"My daughter deserves the best, Mel. I'm so excited for you both." He could tell that as troubled as she was, she meant every word.

When he ended the call, Lynda apologized and told him she couldn't believe her mom called him *Jew-boy*. Then she added, "actually I can," to which he winked and said, "She isn't going to run me off any time soon. That's a promise."

"You say that now," she warned playfully. Then she slid her sunglasses on and stared out the mammoth-sized windshield, adding, "It was sweet, though. What she said about us."

Mel & Lynda at Lake Ella, Tallahassee

CHAPTER FORTY-SIX
NOTHING LESS THAN GRACE

Late afternoon shadows were creeping over the palm fronds by the time Mel pulled the Loft into a spacious rest stop twenty-five miles from Gainesville. He parked between two semis and turned the generator on, preparing for a nap. Both he and Lynda were feeling drowsy, and after stretching their legs outside, they headed to the bedroom to lie down. Though he only planned to rest his eyes for a few minutes, he fell into a deep sleep, a fact he only realized after he awoke.

He turned his head to see Lynda still lying beside him and staring at the low ceiling. Then she rolled over to face him, eyes misty with emotion.

"I think Myrna was just here," she said. Hearing Myrna's name piqued his senses, startling him into full waking consciousness.

"What?"

Lynda rubbed her eyes and yawned. She seemed to still be speaking from that place between dreams and waking.

"I fell asleep and then I woke up – and when I woke up . . . I think she was here," she continued. "Well, I wasn't awake exactly. I think as I began to wake up, I saw, or felt, an energy. Like a shimmering cloud hovering over us."

"You saw Myrna?"

"Not exactly. It was just like when it happened in my living room. I felt her presence, and I knew it was her. Then I heard the words, 'My work here is done.'"

"My work here is done? What does that mean?" He massaged his temples with his thumb and middle finger, something he often did when he needed to think. He felt like each time he'd finally processed the unexplainable things that were happening, some new mystery appeared. He wondered if this would be a new normal.

"Maybe it means you're here." Lynda waved her arm like a tour guide drawing attention to some amazing backdrop. "You're home."

"Tampa?"

"No, with me. Like she knows we're solid now. She's complete with us because... we're complete." Mel's insides felt like a still lake someone tossed a rock into, his thoughts circles that reverberated out, flowing over something hidden beneath. This curious mix of invigoration and stillness stayed with him for the rest of the drive, as if he was standing at the edge of something very important, watching as it was submerged and recreated, and waiting for it to rise into view. If that's indeed what Myrna meant by "home", the rightness of it registered to the bone.

At the end, she'd told him she wanted to go home. But she had to do it alone. He couldn't help her. Now, she was the one who seemed to be helping both he and Lynda find their ways to one another, to a new home they could create together. He had always known how much Myrna loved him. But this? This was a love so tremendous, it could reach beyond the veil of time, of life and death. He was astonished at the miracle, and that he might actually be worthy of it.

If he had prayed for a second chance at love, Myrna had heard him.

And he realized that all of it was something some might chalk up to wishful thinking, to the longing for comfort, or permission even, to move on. To fall in love. Or, even to dream.

And he couldn't say any of that was untrue.

But he also knew, fully and completely, that there was also another truth, a miraculous one that didn't make rational sense. It was nothing less than grace.

It was shortly after sunset when all thirty-four feet of the Loft pulled quietly onto Renellie Drive and lurched to a stop beside the curb in front of Lynda's house. Mel, somehow managing not to block anyone's driveway, cut the engine, and turned all the lights off.

As he stepped down into the balmy breeze blowing through the palms, he was happy to be home. With a sense of serenity mixed with excitement, he was looking forward to embarking on this "adventure" with Lynda, and he was optimistic about the possibilities for the future.

CHAPTER FORTY-SEVEN
THE BIG QUESTIONS

Mel's arrival in Tampa initiated many questions, some little, some big, some predictable, and some that came as a complete surprise.

The first of these questions were small and became evident in the humble train of essential objects and personal effects that traveled between Lynda's house and the Loft, parked thirty miles away in Pinellas County.

A favorite tube of toothpaste, a soft-bristle hair brush, a change of clothes, an overnight satchel. Little things got left behind and were missed. Or, they were remembered and rejoiced over. Sometimes, they were misplaced and forgotten. At the end of the day, these tiny tumults served only to highlight what mattered, which was not where they spent time and what to take. What mattered was being together, which happened mostly at night, and mostly at Lynda's.

It was also after his arrival that murmurs within the RYL community began. These too appeared in the guise of smaller questions. Only later would he fully realize how monumental they were.

They began as off-handed comments, invariably phrased as something harmless someone heard someone else say. They also arrived as questions someone had posed "for Mel's own good."

Was it too soon after Myrna's death for him to begin another relationship? Had he grieved long enough? How long should his grieving period be?

While they were good questions, these well-intentioned murmurs were the last things on Mel's mind. After all, only he could answer them for himself. And, in fact, he already had by virtue of his decisions. Now, he wanted to harness his newfound energy for what seemed like a better cause than wondering how long he should feel sad. So, he preoccupied himself with a different set of questions. He began to wonder how his life changes could galvanize his teaching, the RYL community, and most importantly, his life mission.

One lazy Sunday afternoon, he and Lynda discussed these possibilities over coffee as they sat on Lynda's big, orange sofa. She glanced around, noticing that the room epitomized what her mom might call "well lived in." It was laundry day and the sound of towels fluffing in the dryer provided the only background noise to their conversation.

"The community knows best what it needs, so maybe I could reach out," Mel said. Lynda agreed, and began offering ideas as she reached down, placing a folded t-shirt into the laundry basket. She sighed and carried the basket of folded laundry over to the computer desk, which sat in a little alcove just beyond the sofa. Several stacks of folded t-shirts, socks, and underwear had already accumulated on the top shelf.

"What do you think about a Steering Committee of some kind?" Mel continued from the sofa. She began transferring the laundry stacks from the basket to the shelf.

"Steering Committee?"

"Yeah. We could get together with grads who are committed to the RYL community, with varied backgrounds and experience, and discuss how to improve the community. Set the balls in motion." What he wasn't saying was that he'd realized that he was frustrated. The past few years had shown him that he wanted, and needed, to share responsibility more, not only with the community, but with Cindy. They'd all done a terrific job of pulling together through Myrna's illness and while he travelled, but student enrollment had steadily dropped off. Now, he hoped to brainstorm together for the betterment of the community.

"Like a task force? That's a great idea," Lynda said, her voice light, if a little distracted. Mel had been staying at her house every night for the past few weeks, and while she loved every second of it, her home was also more chaotic. As she hoisted the basket onto her hip, it registered that most of the stacks in it belonged to Mel. She'd noticed before, but it was only now, as she regarded his growing stack of t-shirts and underwear on the computer desk, that she realized, if it was here to stay, love might need a little more room. She left the basket on the floor and headed towards her bedroom with an efficient stride.

From the living room, Mel heard her rummaging around and started thinking about how much he liked her energy and industriousness. Then he heard her call him from the bedroom. Her voice sounded playful but that was normal. This time, though, something about it made his heart stop in a good way.

Before he could let his imagination wander too much, she walked back into the living room with an enthusiastic expression. "Come here, I want to show you something!" Hoping that laundry day and talk of Steering Committees was about to get a lot more interesting, he followed her into the bedroom.

They stopped in front of her dresser as she opened one of its drawers and turned to look at him. Over her shoulder, he noticed the drawer was empty... definitely not what he was expecting.

"What's this?" he asked. Lynda smiled and pointed at the drawer.

"It's for you."

"For me?" In an upsurge of happiness, he embraced her and realized he'd just received the best present in the world from the only person who could give it. "I have an underwear drawer!" he exclaimed.

CHAPTER FORTY-EIGHT
CALCULUS OF GRIEF

Still, even as their romance blossomed, Mel found himself repeatedly needing to field questions from individuals in the RYL community. More murmurs and opinions. One particular opinion began to stand out, gathering unexpected momentum.

It was the opinion that he'd entered a new relationship too soon.

He was no grief expert, and it was possible that for some it was too soon. This is why each time someone reported what "other people" were saying, he listened. Even though he didn't know exactly *who* held this opinion, he believed that they meant well. And though he might have disagreed with their opinions, he chose to view this as an opportunity to honor their feelings. This was the RYL way. Mel expected to ask and be asked uncomfortable questions, because that's where growth began.

One RYL principle is that every individual can empower himself by taking full responsibility for his or her own life. While one cannot control another's behavior, we each are responsible for our own feelings. By examining our own thought patterns and feelings associated with an experience, we can uncover the underlying belief system that created our thoughts or behaviors in the first place. Another person's behavior is merely a *trigger*, which can spark an unconscious belief. By bringing this belief into conscious thought, we now have the power to change it. This process of *redirecting* brings us back full circle to "personal responsibility" while respecting the individual's perspective.

This is why, whenever he caught wind of what he came to refer to as "other people's opinions," he put his teaching hat on.

The truth was that his new relationship was the result of a long and private journey – one of listening to and trusting his heart. It was between him and Upper Management, and he wanted it to stay that way.

A part of him wanted to at least try to explain, but a wiser part resisted. He loved his community, but he wouldn't be a very good leader if his personal life, especially something as intimate and mysterious as the way love showed up, became subject to OPO.

The real question, as he saw it, was why someone would feel the need to control how or when love showed up for anyone else. Or, how they could presume to know what another's grief should look like. What beliefs motivated *them*?

He hoped that asking this question, respectfully and in so many words, would encourage awareness, bring it back around to the practice of RYL principles. He knew that people were still grieving Myrna's death, and in their pain, they were judging him.

So, he put the question back on the anonymous members of the "too soon" camp. "In their opinion," he wondered out loud to anyone who might pass this question along, "how long should I have waited?"

He didn't expect any answers. He trusted that he was the only one who truly knew his feelings, the only one who could know when he was finished grieving and ready to move on with his life. He knew his question was only relevant as an opportunity for them to pause and reflect on their own beliefs. His hope was that they would see the opportunity.

He cleared his mind of these thoughts as he walked up the stairs of his old condo to meet with Carol, his tenant. Part of the RYL family, she was known for her bold, assertive manner. But she had her opinions and, like most people, tended to rely on unexamined assumptions. Mel maintained a friendly relationship with her, but he could never quite shake the impression, perhaps irrational, that he was some kind of admired yet insufficient father figure to her.

It was one of the shadow sides of his position in the community. How do you discourage being put up on the pedestal? It wasn't his model for healthy leadership or even friendship.

Carol answered the door in a cheerful sundress with pink palm trees all over it. Her chunky gold bracelets clinked as he followed her inside. They sat down, nibbled on snacks she'd spread on the table, and chatted. The conversation was proceeding smoothly until she plucked a grape with a bangled hand and raised the issue of people's opinions. Or, more specifically, her opinion.

"Some people are saying things," she started. He knew what she was referring to, and though her comment made him feel a little more guarded, it brought relief. So far, "people's opinions" had come to him second-hand. Finally, he might have the chance to hear directly from someone who believed it was *too soon* for him to be in a relationship.

"What are they saying?" He realized he probably knew the answer, but he wanted to hear what she had to say. He barely managed to get his question out before she answered.

"They don't like it." Her tone was matter-of-fact. "The relationship. They think it's . . . too soon."

Mel chafed when he heard the words. *Too soon.* He asked her what she thought about it.

"According to my psychiatrist, for every five years you're married you should wait one year before you enter another relationship." Mel, who had an accounting background, did the math.

"Myrna and I were married forty-four years. Divided by five, that's almost nine years." He said this as if it were a question.

"Yes," Carol said simply. She appeared to see nothing wrong with the math. Perhaps, he thought, she didn't realize its full implications.

"So, you're saying that I should've waited *nine* years before entering a relationship?"

"Yes," she repeated, as if it was obvious. Her tone grew more decisive and stern. Under such a rule, Mel would be seventy-two years old before he could have another partner. He repressed the urge to scoff, shaking his head instead and changing the subject. It was so preposterous that he wasn't even about to redirect her or help her manage her own beliefs. For the moment, at least, he'd heard all he needed to hear about "other people's opinions."

One thing was certain. When he left the condo, he knew more clearly than ever that the *too soon* question had nothing to do with him.

It was about rules he'd never heard of, personal insecurities and beliefs he wasn't privy to. He couldn't measure sadness and find it lacking, or measure joy and find it excessive. Perhaps some people could, but he couldn't.

And wouldn't. It was against everything he believed in or what he stood for. If the past two years had shown him anything at all, it was that all he could do was lead his own life and take in all the love he possibly could while he still had time.

CHAPTER FORTY-NINE
GOOD-BYES

Never was this clarity more palpable than a few days later while Mel was visiting Aspen to teach RYL. It was Friday evening, and session didn't start until after dinner, so Mel was busy finalizing last-minute details when his phone rang. Seeing his brother's name on the caller ID, he wondered what was going on. Morty, who lived in Toronto, didn't call often.

"It's over," he heard Morty say. "Dad's gone." Solly had been sick for several years, and both his sons knew this had been coming for some time. Still, the blow stunned Mel. He felt his attention narrow, his breath drain out of him.

"When?" he asked. His brother sighed as he answered.

"Last night. Here at the house." Solly had been living with Morty for a few years. And Mel knew how much caretaking could wear on a person. Mel hadn't yet told Solly that Myrna had died. He just felt the stress would've been too great. Now, it was too late.

"Was it . . . peaceful?"

"Yes." Morty told Mel he'd already started planning the funeral. It would be scheduled after the weekend. This meant Mel could finish the course and fly to the funeral. He jotted the date in his planner. Neither of them cried...not unusual, even under these circumstances.

After Mel ended the call, he sat down and stared out the window. A late October snow from the night before was melting. It was too cold for it to melt completely. Whatever was left would harden and freeze once more after the sun went down. It reminded him of his dad, stoic and proud, too sick to enjoy his favorite TV shows or read his treasured newspapers, alone in his silence. Mel had watched too many loved ones suffer, including his father, and he was grateful that his suffering was over.

He thought about how much Solly had taught him over the years. How he'd been the original Iceman. How he'd never stopped grieving for Mel's mother. Solly didn't express his feelings, but Mel learned to accept his father's detached nature, perhaps because they were more alike than they were different. His relationship with his father had shaped him, perhaps even led to his passion and all the principles that upheld it, crystallized in RYL. He knew Solly would never be comfortable in the new world Mel created for himself, but somehow, Solly had helped inspire it. He was grateful to his father for that, and for always taking care of him and loving him, even though Solly stopped short of saying so.

Mel felt the all too familiar pang of grief well up and thought about teaching in the midst of it. When Myrna was sick, neither of them missed a course until the month before she died. It wasn't about a rule or promise that they had made. It was where they wanted to be. Going through that experience taught him that the course room was one of his most essential comforts, and he knew teaching would help him move through the pain of losing Solly.

In the course room, he could be real. He could express his feelings. RYL wasn't only about the student's growth or support. It was about his own as well.

It would've been so easy to shut down and withdraw when tragedy struck. That's what the ego wanted, and for that matter, the common response in society today. But the course room offered an antidote to all who entered it. He could show up with authenticity and tell his truth. In joy or grief he could say, *this is what's happening with me.*

Having the space to express himself with love was such a simple, profound thing. Both he and his students practiced being emotionally transparent – relentlessly. Sometimes, the drive to be authentic felt urgent and elemental, as if it were life itself. It's what enabled him to both reach out and stay grounded when he was in danger of feeling most alone.

After the course and funeral were over, he returned to Tampa, and began the work to get his new Steering Committee off the ground.

Myrna had always cautioned him to stay away from negative energy, so he chose to focus on moving forward in a positive path. He felt more and more hopeful as he charted new directions for the community. Lynda had embraced the opportunity to start a new chapter in her life as a co-instructor, and they scheduled an RYL for Couples course for February. He worked and slept at her house more and more, and he traveled less to the Loft. Finally, one night after dinner, Lynda looked up at him and asked what had become all too obvious.

"When did we decide to live together?" He looked around, delight shooting like stars at the sudden realization that their relationship had grown so much, without either of them even trying. His answer arose effortlessly.

"Well, whenever it was, it was most definitely not *too soon.*"

CHAPTER FIFTY
OTHER PEOPLE'S OPINIONS

It was the best kind of story, the kind that belonged to everyone and no one. And he'd told it hundreds of times.

The setting was always the same. Someone who was struggling would land in the RYL course room. They'd share their story, often weeping at truths they'd rarely spoken aloud. And, when the student was able to hear it, and if it felt appropriate, Mel would tell the starfish story.

"One afternoon, a young man was walking along the ocean and saw thousands of starfish washed ashore. Further away he saw an old man, walking slowly and stooping down often, picking up one starfish after another and tossing each one gently into the ocean.

Why are you throwing starfish into the ocean? the young man asked.

Because the sun is up and the tide is going out, and if I don't throw them in they will die, the old man shouted over the wind.

But, old man, don't you realize there are miles and miles of beach and starfish all along it! You can't possibly save them all, you can't even save a tenth of them. In fact, even if you work all day, your efforts won't make any difference at all, the young man insisted.

The old man listened as he bent down to pick up another starfish and toss it into the sea. Then he replied.

It made a difference to that one."

Every student got their turn as the starfish in the RYL course room. Honoring the theme of this story, one starfish at a time, Mel and Cindy were dedicated to help one soul at a time. Their organization was *mission*-driven, not profit-driven —a mission *To create global oneness and a new way of living in the world through profound learning experiences one soul at a time.*

This is why he was excited when the RYL Steering Committee became a reality and scheduled its first official meeting.

He hoped it would give him deeper insight into the evolving needs of the community, which now numbered several hundred grads in the Tampa Bay area alone. He also looked forward to being in closer dialogue with the Committee members as individuals, and to discovering how they could all work together to reach those "starfish" that might wash up on the beach.

Until now, they had relied on word-of-mouth and face-to-face networking to recruit new students. It was old school, and although it was most effective, it also took a considerable amount of time and energy. Leads came through graduates, many of them eager to share RYL with friends and family. But with Myrna's diagnosis and the subsequent upheaval in his life, Mel's focus had shifted from meeting with potential students to tending to Myrna's needs. It had taken a toll on enrollment, as the numbers of students had dropped steadily over the last two years. He was interested to hear new ideas for marketing and recruiting to help revitalize the business.

He realized that he had taken on the bulk of the load, and it was time to ask for help. He didn't want the continuance of "the Work", and the ability to carry out his life purpose, to be that vulnerable to changes in his personal life. He wanted to increase community involvement and support by gaining their feedback and input, and he hoped to inspire a commitment in the Community to keep this transformative work going.

It was time to share the responsibility.

What he didn't yet fully comprehend was how the discomfort over his new love had started to fester, creating dissension within a part of the community. It would seep into all his good intentions and well-laid plans, and taint the starfish walk that comprised the core and purpose of his life.

The first real signs of tension appeared after Mel published Lynda's bio on the website, announcing her as Mel's co-instructor for the upcoming Couple's Course. Instructor bios always went on the site months before the scheduled course date so that they could start recruiting students. But shortly after the bio went live, Mel received a call from Cindy, asking why Lynda's bio was on the website.

Taken aback, Mel reclined in his office chair and stared at the ceiling. He'd actually already run this by her, so Cindy knew about Lynda teaching. She also knew it was routine to put all instructor bios on the website.

"What do you mean?" he asked her. He felt truly confused. When Cindy replied, her voice was formal but polite.

"Some people have reported to me that her bio is on the website. They don't think it's professional." Here they were again, Mel thought to himself. Other People's Opinions.

"What are they saying exactly? That the bio is live or that it's not professional?" Cindy hesitated.

"Both." Mel was deflated. There was no way to address this since he didn't know who said it or what context it was said in. He also couldn't tell if Cindy agreed. Either way, he was starting to feel genuinely picked on, and he couldn't help but feel increasingly protective of Lynda.

"Well, I don't know what to say except I've been publishing instructor bios for ten years, and it's as professional as any I've seen." When he asked her exactly what was unprofessional about Lynda's bio, she claimed it was that Lynda's bio stated she was in a relationship with Mel. This also made no sense. Couples course instructors were often real-life couples and many were even married, as he and Myrna were all the years they'd taught together.

"Lynda hasn't even taught yet. Why is her bio on the website at all?" Cindy pressed. Frustrated, Mel took a moment to control his tone before responding.

"Cindy, I have to start recruiting and enrolling students for the course now, and potential students need to be able to go to our website and read about the instructors. This is the way we've always done it."

"But –"

"And there's never been a problem before." They were quiet as Mel tried and failed to make sense of her behavior. She'd never expressed concern over a bio before.

Only Lynda's.

"I just feel you should've asked my permission before putting the bio up." Mel felt incredulous as he was reminded of the time Cindy berated Lynda for discussing her new relationship. Cindy played the permission card then, too. He and Cindy had always had a good rapport, and he dreaded the idea of losing it. But things were starting to feel less friendly, and he didn't know what to do. He lived by the teaching that *it's better to be close than to be right*. He didn't want to argue with her, to make her "wrong," especially when he wasn't even sure what the objection was about.

"How would I know to do that? I've always been the one who was responsible for putting the instructor bios on the website, and you've never asked me to run them by you until now." At this, Cindy's voice turned plaintive.

"Don't get me wrong. I'm just reporting what others are saying. I feel I could've helped prevent this if I'd been consulted. I could've made . . . suggestions."

"Suggestions?"

"For instance, there's a similar Couple's Course in Orlando. Maybe you should look at those instructor bios. They're good models." Mel stared at the ceiling. It was impossible to be business partners with someone for ten years and not have disagreements. Neither of them was perfect. But this kind of senseless conflict was uncharted territory. He felt judged and misunderstood and felt himself growing silent and shutting down. He felt like she was questioning his integrity.

He tended to withdraw when he felt overwhelmed or discouraged. He'd done that since his Iceman days.

When they ended the call, he thought back to the August course. He remembered his elation when he embraced Lynda in front of everyone. At the time, it felt like his first public affirmation of their romance. So many people congratulated him afterwards, both of them. There was such a positive response, and he'd felt grateful for the love and support of the community.

But after this conversation with Cindy, he wondered, *Have I missed something?* As he replayed scenes from the weekend in his mind, he began to see something he'd been too preoccupied to notice at the time. Those who'd hung back and remained silent now slowly came into focus. *Don't-get-in-a-relationship-for-nine-years* Carol was one of them.

Mel was already aware that their friendship had changed. Now, he began to see that he was not only experiencing perplexing behavior from Cindy, but from Carol, and others as well. And it all had started shortly after they'd learned about his new relationship.

He reviewed their reasoning, all the subtle ways they'd quietly communicated their disapproval through others. He hadn't grieved enough, they thought. He hadn't considered the needs of the community, another thought.

How could that be? What were the expectations? The RYL course taught that people should be free to live truthfully and authentically. He'd dedicated many years to practicing non-judgement and self-acceptance – and teaching others to do the same. How could his living his own truth be so uncomfortable for others? Even to those who professed to share the same values he did? Especially when they hadn't traveled his journey or walked in his shoes? Now, he was the one asking questions.

Had he been naive for not seeing this sooner? For not anticipating it?

He cared deeply for many of these people and respected all of them as fellow travelers on life's path. And he was always available to help them examine the beliefs that led to judgement or unhappiness, even in this matter. He hated feeling misunderstood and wished they could appreciate the miracles and beauty that had brought his second love to him. And he refused to defend himself, or the fact that he'd fallen in love.

His personal life was not a democracy. It wasn't open to consensus rule. He'd never promised that it would be, or that anyone else would get to decide the right time for him to fall in love again. The fact that they might believe they did confounded him. He realized being a leader subjected him to scrutiny, but it was also why he had to stand his ground.

Prejudice, gossip, and Other People's Opinions were not what RYL was about.

And if he had anything to do with it, they never would.

CHAPTER FIFTY-ONE
WHAT STRENGTH FEELS LIKE

Lynda threw her suitcase on the bed and began making a mental list of what to pack. She was spending the post-Christmas holiday in the mountains with Mel and the kids, and after everything that had been going on, she had to admit she needed a holiday.

Life with Mel had been nurturing and joyful, especially after he officially moved in. And when she thought about their romance, it seemed nothing less than magical. Fate even.

But like everything else, even fairy tales have their dark sides.

Even though she disagreed, she could understand why some people might think it was too soon for Mel to get into a relationship after becoming a widower. Even her dad had expressed concern, but not because he was worried about Mel's character. It was because he knew both of them had recently lost relationships. He'd warned her that the romance might've been a rebound for both of them. But her dad trusted her to follow her heart and make her own decisions, even though he'd seen her make plenty of mistakes in the past. But those mistakes were a path to learning, and the reason she was able to be an equal partner to Mel now. Through her past relationships she had learned more about herself, more about what she wanted in a relationship, and equally important, what she was no longer willing to accept. And, she believed she was worthy of the love she sought.

She knew now that she hadn't been following her heart when she settled for less than she wanted or deserved. She was following empty hope. Her life had a true path. She knew that following her heart – trusting her heart – would lead her there.

And it had.

Still, it was increasingly clear that some people took issue with that path.

She respected that the grief process was individual. It didn't follow a program or a timeline. It also seemed to be its own entity, a creature no one could predict or force into some kind of pattern. Because of this, she had decided to wait out the *too soon* camp. They weren't necessarily wrong about grief, but they were wrong about her and Mel. She was confident that in time, they would see the strong partnership that they were building together...feel the love and respect that they had for one another as well as the whole RYL community.

But while she waited, the discord only grew stronger. And she and Mel became more frustrated – not only with the situation, but with trying to figure out how best to manage it.

She and Mel had looked up the model bios Cindy pointed out. What they discovered proved to be both laughable and unsettling.

There was nothing "more professional" about these bios. Or, bio, as it were, since there was only one combined for the two of them. And they made no secret about their relationship. Why would they, since being coupled was a reasonable qualification to teach relationship skills to other couples.

While Mel and Lynda had posted individual headshots, as well as separate bios, Cindy's model couple posed in an embrace, smiling out from a single photograph. Their joint bio introduced them as a couple while light-heartedly discussing their togetherness in their relationship. Lynda had been careful to keep hers strictly professional, making no mention of her personal life except that she was in a relationship with Mel.

As she compared her bio with theirs, it didn't fail to escape her that her picture was now placed where Myrna's once was.

She wondered if this was the real problem with the bio.

She could see that some people were having a difficult time accepting the changes in Mel's life, and even more now with the changes in the RYL couples retreat. She tried to put herself in their position, to see the situation from their perspective. Could it be that some members of the community weren't complete with their own grieving process? What were their beliefs about death and dying that may be influencing their behavior? And, if *they* weren't ready to move on, she reasoned, it only made sense that they might question whether Mel was ready to move on.

Lynda was an optimist. She wanted to believe in and see the best in people, herself included. Because she'd worked so conscientiously at developing into a person who could keep an open mind and seek to understand rather than judge others, it was all too easy for her to assume her fellow assistants were the same way.

For the past six years, the RYL course room had been a place where she felt accepted and loved just as she was. Now, she wondered if she'd been seeing the RYL community through "rose-colored glasses."

The community was values-based, and everyone in it shared a commitment to self-development. Nevertheless, some of them were further along in their "process" than others, and with the loss of Myrna, the community had entered uncharted territory. Lynda suggested to Mel that they find a way to help the community process their grief, to shift the focus from judgment to personal responsibility. While Mel agreed that there was a growing undercurrent of disharmony in the community, he was uncomfortable with challenging people in the community when it came to his personal life. He didn't feel the need to justify himself or his choices.

A part of her yearned to explain the magic of exactly how things happened...how their friendship of six years had budded into something more on July fourth, was nurtured by Upper Management with Myrna's assistance, and had bloomed into a loving, committed partnership. Then they would understand.

In the end, Lynda bowed to his experience, trusting that he knew how best to respond to the community he helped create.

RYL was her home, but she could no longer deny that it was portending ripples of discord she seemed to be able to do nothing about. All she could do was keep living her truth. She had faith that, eventually, they would find acceptance. All her life, she'd given more credence to Other People's Opinions than her own. RYL had taught her to be "inner-directed," to trust in her inner wisdom. And although it made her feel anxious, she wanted to do it differently this time.

As if from a trance, Lynda looked up and realized she'd been sitting on her bed staring into space. She hadn't even started to pack. She stood up, and mindful of the winter weather in the mountains, started to gather turtlenecks and sweaters, tossing them in her suitcase.

As she did, she thought of Carol, who she'd once considered a good friend. But Lynda had only heard about Carol's confrontational conversation with Mel because he told her. Carol never mentioned a thing to her. In fact, she didn't hear much from Carol these days at all, which made her sad.

She never expected that falling in love would cost her friendships. Was she naive in believing that her friends in the RYL community would support her and be happy for her?

In the sadness, she felt that old familiar angst in her belly. The thought pattern installed long ago by her mother, who used criticism and disapproval to control her, the one that told her love was conditional and that she wasn't good enough, ran in the back of her mind like an old cassette tape.

She would warn Lynda not to eat this or she'd get fat. Not to wear that or she wouldn't look pretty. Never to disagree with her or face punishment. Lynda was her first-born, her baby, her *everything*. Yet her mother treated her as if Lynda lived to make *her* happy, and though Lynda tried, it was never enough. Though she wasn't conscious of it at the time, Lynda created a belief that if she wanted to be loved, she had to give up what *she* wanted, and sometimes, a little piece of herself.

It wasn't until she was an adult that she realized that her mom was operating from her own twisted belief system, even if she wanted the best for Lynda. She was training Lynda how to be successful in a world where men held the power, how to be a woman in the world her mother grew up in. This was her mother's truth, but in the end, it taught Lynda to put herself last, to get love by pleasing others, by valuing their opinions over her own.

In RYL, Lynda learned that she could change the beliefs that created her sadness. It was her mom's inability or unwillingness to be reflective that drove Lynda into her own desires to do just that. To find true power.

Lynda shivered in the December chill, pulled a sweatshirt from the suitcase, and pulled it on.

She could handle this, she told herself, as she allowed her concerns over the community conflict, and her own triggered wounds, to subside. The voice of doubt, once so loud, waned. In its place she heard Mel's voice, whose love seemed to expand by the day.

And she heard that of her own, which sounded fresh, different somehow.

It told her, very clearly, *Life is good! Trust in the Process. I love and accept myself.* She stared out her window at the balmy Florida day and leaned in to hear this new voice.

Maybe this is what strength feels like, it whispered.

CHAPTER FIFTY-TWO
98% FEARLESS

"When I was a teenager, we used to come up here for family vacation. I fell in love with the mountains." Lynda propped her feet up and gazed at the fire glowing and popping in the fireplace. She was sitting beside Mel on a couch in their vacation rental. The earthy smell of wood smoke fused with the rich wine as she lifted her glass to take a sip.

"It would be hard not to," he said. "I've always liked them, too. I even dreamt of living in this area when I was younger." They'd spent the day strolling the sidewalks of quaint North Carolina mountain towns with the kids, popping in and out of gift shops crammed with cinnamon candles, needlepoints, and black bear trinkets. The black bear tchotchke was as abundant as starfish tchotchke in Florida. And though she loved the area, even Lynda had to agree when the kids complained they'd seen enough "country crafts," and they'd returned to the cabin for a warm meal of homemade stew.

"Really? Me, too." Lynda had no idea they shared the dream of living in the same place. The Smoky Mountains were famous for their magnificent, blue mountains, though weather and fog dulled them this time of year. Still, even under the chrome colored skies, Lynda reveled in the season.

"Reminds me of home," he added. Mel was referring to the Laurentian Mountains north of Montreal, where he spent weekends as a teenager with Myrna's family and later vacationed with their own family in the summer months. He was telling her how the Laurentians were one of the oldest ranges in the world when Billy followed Brandy and Nick into the living area. She regarded the young couple as they sat on a second couch beside the fireplace. Billy plopped into a large armchair nearby. Looking at her kids, she thought her heart might burst.

"Look how cute they are," she exclaimed, quiet enough so they wouldn't overhear. Mel smiled. He knew the young couple had put energy into figuring out how their long-distance relationship would work and were in the final stages of deciding, very methodically, that Nick would soon transfer to Florida State to be closer to Brandy. He let his head fall towards Lynda's.

"Look how cute we are," he said in her ear. She giggled, sharing how proud she was of Billy, who was doing so much better than he was six months ago. "Turns out you were right, mom," Mel said. "RYL helped him after all."

Lynda nodded in agreement. Then, she switched the subject back to the mountains.

"I want to experience all four seasons," she said. "Something other than hurricane season, that is." Mel popped his eyebrow up inquisitively. He asked her what else she wanted.

Lynda appreciated this skill of his, how he could seamlessly blend coaching and just being. She continued talking, weaving her dreams and hopes together into a new vision that felt more clear and true than ever, perhaps because it created a future that included him. Mel listened, deep in thought. Then, he asked a follow-up question.

"Did you just propose to me?" He said it as if it were a joke. But its truth also startled Lynda. She stopped and thought about their conversation – sharing her hopes and dreams of the future – one in which she saw them building a life together. She suddenly felt a little vulnerable, as if she might somehow reveal too much. She looked into Mel's eyes, a little unsteady. Then, she spoke.

"I guess I did." Another joke. Another truth. Mel felt it even as he savored the note of humor. He liked this way they had, of occupying starkly different emotional spaces at once. It felt easy.

"I'm open. I think it could work between us." Hearing her own response, Lynda felt a mixture of shock, joy, and unease. Confused, she retreated into thought, though she didn't fully understand why she felt the need.

Mel, sensing her reservation, asked her if she was "sure."

She knew the most important questions were often the most difficult, and she struggled to find her answer. Perhaps it was the elation of standing on the precipice of a dream-come-true that also opened her to the small, fragile part of herself that still protected itself, kept itself separate. It had been hurt too often. Then a number rose up in her awareness. Its specificity made it seem all the more random.

"98%. I feel 98% sure." Mel didn't skip a beat.

"What's the 2% about?" he asked. She knew he was asking for her benefit more than his, to help draw her closer to her truth. She didn't know why she, or why anyone, held themselves back, hid slices of their hearts. This part of herself felt momentous. Her emotions began to clamor, as if she walked a tightrope and might stumble into tears at any moment. Mel's gaze held her steady.

"I don't know. Time, maybe?" As she said this, she heard laughter from the other couch and saw Billy goofing around in the corner of her eye. Then Mel asked the question that broke her open.

"What's the fear about?" She hadn't mentioned fear. But she didn't need to.

"I guess I'm afraid . . . what if it doesn't work out?" She felt as if this question held all the pieces of her heart, all the pieces that had been taken, that she'd given away, that she'd lost.

"But what if," he asked gently, "it works out beyond our wildest dreams?" The tears that had been welled up behind her eyes began falling. She felt them turning the dashed hopes of her past into a vista of possibility that waited only for her to receive it.

Had they really just discussed marriage?

The sound of Billy loudly clearing his throat pulled her from her reverie. His face was aglow as he stood in front of the fireplace like a seasoned ringmaster waiting for the circus crowd to quiet down. Brandy and Nick, who'd been luxuriating in their own bubble, emerged, turning their faces towards him. When all eyes were on him, Billy started belting out a famous lament.

"All by myself, don't wanna be all by myself!" They all recognized the song as soon as they heard it and began laughing uproariously. Billy sang the entire song and when he was finished, bowed to his adoring fans, who clapped and took his song as a hint that it was time to get back into a group. Lynda's tears disappeared.

Was it the warm light of the fire or the cleansing laughter from Billy's joke? Was it Brandy's and Nick's young love or Mel's gentle questions? She didn't know the reason, but something had shifted.

Her fear had dissolved, and she felt nothing but tenderness when she recognized how good life was. Better than she had imagined.

Even the dusty, wooden black bear rearing up on its hind legs beside the fireplace couldn't take that away.

CHAPTER FIFTY-THREE
VALENTINE'S DAY

Over the next couple of months, the wisps of conflict that had appeared in autumn quietly gained momentum. Unexpected complications and impasses littered Mel's days, and navigating them left him increasingly stressed. On the surface, they seemed to involve details. The mundane activities of planning future courses. Logistics. Schedules. But these practical matters merely masked what became increasingly impossible to ignore – the growing tension over his relationship with Lynda.

Mel's disagreement with Cindy over the professionalism of Lynda's bio had become a protracted argument.

When he confronted Cindy over the fact that her "model" instructors were open about their relationship in their bios, she responded blandly that she didn't "go that deep." Did she mean she hadn't actually read them?

In the past, he would've turned the other cheek at this behavior, but he was starting to see that it wasn't as benign as he'd thought. After all, this was about more than his relationship with Lynda or his business partnership – or even his friendship with Cindy. It was about the spirit of integrity, which was the very foundation of their teachings. "Love others, and work on yourself" was about getting really honest with yourself and focusing on your own feelings and thoughts in a given situation – not judging or blaming others. Mel did more than just teach RYL, he *lived* it. He practiced the principles on a daily basis, and when grads called for help with a problem in their lives, he "redirected" them, gently guiding them to a place of acceptance and non-judgement.

This spirit was one he thought he and Cindy shared. Now, he was beginning to wonder. *Why hadn't Cindy "redirected" those who were judging him when she had the opportunity?* His disillusionment caused him to take a good hard look at the imbalance between he and Cindy, and he realized it had started long before Myrna's death or his relationship with Lynda. And, for the sake of keeping the peace, he had never confronted her. How had he let it go so far?

Finding teachers for out-of-town courses also caused unforeseen issues.

He made every effort to find a co-teacher for the upcoming March RYL course in California. Cindy wasn't able to travel that weekend, and initially he had it covered by his daughter Melanie. However, the course date coincided with the first anniversary of Myrna's death, and Melanie had a change of plans when her brothers asked her to meet in Tampa to visit their mother's grave. Mel understood and respected her decision, and if the course hadn't been scheduled, he'd probably be standing right beside them. Still, he was content with honoring the anniversary in one of the places he and Myrna loved best: the RYL course room.

So he'd been canvassing for qualified instructors for weeks. He needed a co-instructor, or he'd be obliged to cancel the course. Although he could easily instruct the course on his own, it was customary to have both male and female leads for each course.

As the date approached and there were only three students enrolled, he considered calling it off, realizing that even if it proceeded, he'd take a financial loss. But like the man throwing starfish into the sea one by one, Mel was dedicated to helping people whenever he could.

It matters to that one.

As the course drew near, he thought of a solution to his dilemma.

Lynda.

She was already flying out to assist for the weekend, she had years of experience in the course room, and she was comfortable in front of groups. It just made sense, especially since no one else was available. He would do most of the teaching, and she would be there for support, mostly holding space for "feminine energy." Ideally, she should be formally certified, but since this was a small, out-of-town course, he saw no reason she couldn't substitute for this *one* course, if it could prevent it from being cancelled.

But it wasn't only about being expedient. He believed in her.

Lynda, however, wasn't so convinced. She was happy to help, but she didn't want to make waves, and she only agreed to "sit up front" with him if Cindy gave her approval. It was important that they be united in this decision.

When he called Cindy to run it by her, he anticipated some resistance, but she surprised him. After a brief discussion, she simply said, "I don't think she's ready, but I trust your instincts." In light of the rough spot they'd been in, he really appreciated her support, and told her so.

He thought their agreement signaled the end of the matter, but she would surprise him in this, too.

A few days later, he got another call. Cindy didn't sound happy.

"Mel, I need to pass along some information I've heard from some grads. They're expressing concern." He had now grown accustomed to receiving information third party, and he felt uneasy. There would be no names, he'd have no idea what was actually being said or by how many people, and it would involve Lynda. He gritted his teeth. "It's not personal, mind you. They don't think Lynda should be teaching in California."

"Why?"

"They think you're showing favoritism."

"Favoritism?" Mel was incredulous. He couldn't believe that any of them would actually think this if they knew the circumstances of *why* Lynda agreed to substitute in the first place.

"Did you explain to them that this was an exception made due to circumstances? That she is standing in for you and for others who weren't available, and that if she didn't, we'd have to cancel the course?" Silence on the other end.

"Not exactly. I told them I'd talk to you about it." So, he thought, she wasn't going to have his back after all.

"You said that you trusted my instincts, that you would support my decision," Mel countered.

"Well, I changed my mind."

Mel was confounded. *What was he going to do now?* "What do you expect me to do? I've already committed to the course in California now."

Cindy would offer no solutions, reminding him that she was just the messenger sharing what she had heard. Refusing to be intimidated, Mel chose to remain committed to the students and dedicated to the cause. He had given his word.

The monthly meeting for the new Steering Committee took place at Lynda's house on a blustery, moonless evening. It was Valentine's Day. As Lynda glanced at her watch and busied herself with last minute tidying, she couldn't help but feel a sense of foreboding.

A conversation earlier in the week with Christi, one of her RYL friends, was one reason. Christi had mentioned in passing that she and her husband might attend the meeting. This struck Lynda as odd, since they'd declined to participate in the Committee when Mel had initially invited them. That was before the New Year.

Christi had always been tirelessly helpful so at the time, Lynda figured Christi just wanted to be supportive. But as she waited for the committee members to arrive, she couldn't help but wonder if Christi's comment was related to something Mel had shared with her.

Apparently, when he was finalizing the meeting agenda with Cindy, she'd asked him if he was "sure he wanted to have it at Lynda's." Both she and Mel had dismissed Cindy's question as her routine resistance to anything "Lynda." But now, Lynda couldn't get it out of her head.

Something was up.

She was aware of the disquiet over her substituting in the March course, on top of the other complaints and opinions, but it wasn't only that. People seemed to be treating them differently, too.

Some people simply didn't socialize with her and Mel as much anymore. And a handful had even left the community. While their reasons for leaving varied, Lynda suspected that the overall contention, and in particular, their own discomfort, played a part. Perhaps the RYL community wasn't the safe haven from rumor and conflict they had envisioned it to be.

Lynda knew she and Mel still had many friends, like Christi and her husband Ed, who'd been very supportive of their relationship. But even with them, the controversy was an elephant in the room. All things considered, tonight's meeting, which would've once felt warm and comfortable, filled her with anxiety. But she'd chosen her position and she would stand by it, come what may.

Lynda went to the kitchen to rinse some glasses. She stood there at the sink, allowing the warm water splashing from the faucet to soothe her as she reminded herself that the RYL community was like any other. It was imperfect, and full of imperfect people, herself included. But those same imperfections made it stronger. And there would always be people who got along and people who didn't.

A fundamental RYL teaching was that everyone had a right to feel the way they feel, even when those around them didn't understand. So, she accepted those who didn't approve of her relationship with Mel. She couldn't stop anyone from expressing their feelings or choosing to withdraw from her. And she didn't want to. However, the flip side of that teaching was that everyone had the obligation to take full responsibility for their own feelings, and avoid blaming someone else for them.

She felt like some people were blaming her for their feelings, instead of taking responsibility and talking about them with her. And they were reacting by complaining, avoiding her, or even taking a break from the community.

Still, she couldn't let go of the hope that most of them would adjust. She was hurting, but she knew it was necessary to give people the time they needed to resolve their feelings.

As she stared out the window into the inky night, she reminded herself that at the end of the day, perhaps a day just like this, they all cared about the same things. Didn't they?

Lynda startled when she heard the doorbell. Wiping her hands on a dishtowel, she hurried from the kitchen to greet the first arrivals.

CHAPTER FIFTY-FOUR
SETUPS

Mel stood in the doorway, but when she glanced over his shoulder, she saw five people. Christi and her husband Ed were there, along with another couple. And Cindy.

But none in the group, except for Cindy, were actually Steering Committee members, and Mel would've told her about any unexpected guests. That meant he didn't know they were coming either. Her anxiety ratcheted up.

As the small group poured into the room and began exchanging polite greetings, they gave off the distinct impression of cohesion, as if they'd arrived together, and for a reason she didn't understand. Mel's bearing reflected similar misgivings. His brows were furrowed, and he seemed more controlled than usual. Stiffer.

While the rest of the committee members arrived, she realized how "on guard" they were both feeling, and she felt a sense of dread cascade through her body. She hadn't been imagining things earlier. Something *was* off. And she could tell by the look on Mel's face that he knew it, too.

Why were these people at this meeting? What were they told and by whom?

"As you know, we're here to talk about how to increase enrollment." Lynda was sitting on the big, orange couch listening to Cindy commence the meeting. Cindy was as poised as ever but something about her voice seemed more circumspect, sad even. "I've invited Debbie to mediate for us as we tackle some of the deeper issues that could relate to enrollment."

Debbie, already making her way to a giant paper pad propped on an easel, flashed a cautious smile. She was an ambitious woman who professed to inspire happiness in others but now, Lynda found her smile less than encouraging. And she noticed something else. Debbie's hands were empty. She wasn't holding the agenda.

Mel's gaze, normally open and inviting, flickered from Debbie to Lynda as Debbie began speaking. His eyes turned steely and dark.

"We've come together because we all love the wonderful community we've built, and we want to see it grow and flourish. And I know I speak for all of us when I say that we all love and respect Mel and Cindy, and this is why it's important to come together and discuss these sensitive matters that seem to be affecting us all." Debbie's voice sounded tin-like. Mel looked around the room, taking stock of the expressions, ranging from veiled to startled, that surrounded him. Cindy's own expression appeared wan, washed out, and she wouldn't meet his eyes. Then he heard Debbie say his name.

"Some of us have felt that there's a disconnect between Mel and Cindy, a rupture of some kind." Here, Debbie paused for effect. "So tonight, we're going off-topic so we can use this time to pull in and support them. Now, if it's okay with everyone, I'm going to touch on areas of concern before we talk about how to best support RYL." No one granted or withheld permission, so Debbie continued. Mel felt a rock sink in his stomach. Whatever was coming was not going to be good. He wondered what the source of Debbie's "concern" actually was as he watched her regard Cindy with obvious sympathy.

"I need to start by saying that we all love and support Mel. We know that he has had a challenging year, and we've become concerned that it has clouded his judgement, and therefore affected his decisions. It has led to upset in the community, and we feel it is time to address it as a group." Debbie was normally articulate, but on this occasion, her words seemed overly precise. It felt as if she'd carefully planned them.

Mel couldn't believe what he was hearing. *Was she attributing the valid issue between him and Cindy to his lack of judgement?*

"One of these decisions concerns Mel publishing an instructor bio without consulting Cindy." She avoided saying Lynda's name, even though she was right there in the room. As soon as Mel heard this, he knew Cindy was at the root of Debbie's vainglorious speech. His hackles, already raised, turned spiky with the first surges of anger. Now he had no doubts about the nature of this meeting.

He felt like he was being attacked.

He looked at his friend Bill, who sat only a few feet away from him. When Bill became an instructor, he'd put Bill's bio on the website without consulting Cindy, too...just like every other instructor in the history of their partnership. It had never been a problem before.

"Then there's the issue with the March course in California," Debbie said, persisting in her pretense of speaking to and for everyone. According to her presentation, Mel also went behind Cindy's back when he chose Lynda to teach with him. Of course, this couldn't be further from the truth. He'd consulted Cindy, and she'd agreed, information that clearly was being omitted tonight.

He felt his gall rise as he watched Cindy's eyes turn misty. He repressed the urge to defend himself, to tell *his* side of the story. And no one was asking him for an explanation or giving him a chance to respond. He felt he was on trial, and he was guilty before proven innocent.

Mel still didn't know who most of the concerned people Debbie spoke of were, but whoever shared Debbie's narrative had their own reasons. Yet, none had made an attempt to talk with him before issuing their own judgments or assessments of his decisions. He felt betrayed.

"This bears on how instructors get chosen and when. It seems that this disconnect might have caused Mel to display partiality in the selection process." Mel sat in shock as Cindy's lip begin to quiver, and she sniffled as if to hold back emotion. "None of us want this negative energy to continue to affect our precious community. Or, its leaders." Debbie finally grew quiet, allowing people to digest her arguments. The room felt heavy and burdened. Then she turned towards Mel.

"Mel, now that these issues have been aired, and knowing that we do this in the spirit of love and understanding, would you like to tell us how you feel?" She sounded like a twelve-stepper leading an intervention. He swallowed his anger, hurt, and disgust.

"I feel like this is a setup," he said simply. He needed time to process it all, and he felt his energy and will spiral downwards, like water circling a drain. He felt himself retreating within, and knew he'd be unable or unwilling to process anything else that was said. He just wanted the charade to end and for everyone to get out of his house. With the exception of Cindy's sniffles, the room was silent.

Another member, attempting to understand, asked Mel why he was so angry. Mel regarded him, saddened by the sudden realization that some of the attendees had absolutely no idea what any of this was about, and flailing in their ignorance, were actually trying to help. How could he explain what was really going on to them? He sighed and shook his head. As angry as he felt with Cindy, he didn't want to make her wrong and call her out in front of this group. He wouldn't betray their partnership like that. He would handle it respectfully and privately.

After that, a few more people spoke about their dedication and support for the community. They didn't know what else to say. Debbie turned to Cindy, who was staring down at her lap.

"Cindy, do you want to tell us how you're feeling?" Cindy wiped her nose.

"I just feel so . . . sad." The tension seemed to deepen and hung heavy in the air. No one moved to comfort Cindy, so she sat forlornly, blotting her tears away. As Mel watched her, he

JOURNEY OF THE HEART   237

didn't doubt that she believed she was sad. It was perhaps the most ironic truth of the night, for he didn't doubt how painful it was for her to watch her actions unfold. She probably didn't even totally understand how her own actions, or lack thereof, had led them all here to this moment.

He ached as he wondered for the first time if this might actually tear the community apart. It was a great feat to build anything worthwhile in this world, especially a truly safe place, a refuge from the storms of life.

But he and Cindy had managed it together. And within their community, many of them had thrived. Now, he felt it was being tainted. And if it continued, he knew many involved would lose hope, their longing to be a part of something greater than themselves shaken. Weakened by disillusionment, their faith in others, and in themselves, would suffer.

And without hope, without trust, who were we?

Deep down, he knew he'd played a part. He promised himself he'd figure out what that was and face it.

He eyed the people sitting around him. Students, instructors, peers, friends. Most of them looked either concerned or confused. Lynda had remained quietly observing most of the meeting, and even though she was angry and confused, she couldn't help but feel sorry for Cindy. Regardless of the part Cindy had played in the evening's objective, she seemed genuinely sad, and very alone. None of the people around her offered her any comfort, and in her own discomfort, Lynda stood up, walked over, and kneeling on the floor beside Cindy, took her hand.

Damn, Mel thought as he watched Lynda holding Cindy's hand. Here she was in her own house listening to this charade, comforting the person who created the drama. He felt his resolve solidify as he watched the two inconceivably different women holding hands.

It was up to him to rectify the situation.

After being prompted by Debbie, Mel reluctantly agreed to reflect on the meeting as well as his anger, and the meeting began to break up. After everyone left, Mel finally found himself standing beside the only person he could bear to look at. As he shut the door and looked at Lynda, he saw his own question forming in her eyes.

What the hell just happened?

CHAPTER FIFTY-FIVE
PURSUITS

"I still don't understand why some of those people were here! Someone had to invite them...was it Cindy?" Lynda sat cross-legged on the bed looking at Mel. He shrugged in reply.

"All I know is that I haven't felt like Cindy has had my back for some time. But I thought that was between me and her. I never considered it might come to this. I'm seeing a side of her I didn't know existed."

"I still can't believe it. At the very least, she had to know what was planned tonight, and I just cannot understand why."

Lynda tried to make sense of her emotions, anger, sadness, betrayal, and confusion swirling within her. It was disbelief, shock even, that overrode them all.

"So many people look up to her." Her voice grew more fragile. "I do . . . or, did." She wanted to cry. She felt like she was in a nightmare putting the pieces of a horrible puzzle together and she couldn't wake up. She kept reliving Debbie's arguments, seeing Cindy's sadness. Small flashes of memory and bits of conversation from the past six months came to her. Things she should've seen but didn't. Things she should've taken seriously but dismissed. All of this had been brewing, and there she'd been again, closing her eyes and hoping for the best. What could she have done differently?

Throughout it all, both she and Mel had stayed quiet. They hadn't explained or defended themselves. It had taken them a while to even wonder if they should. Would that have helped?

"Why didn't you say anything tonight? Why didn't you defend yourself?" she asked suddenly, an edge in her voice. "Don't you think it's time people know the truth?"

"I can tell you're upset. Is it with me, or with them?" Mel was redirecting her. It grated on her nerves.

"I'm upset with them. I feel like I'm losing a huge part of my world. But I'm disappointed with you." He asked her why. "Because you haven't once tried to set this all straight. You're the leader, or one of them, and you could say something."

Mel closed his eyes as he took this in. Had this been *his part*? Had he avoided when he should've confronted? Should he have said something, fought back? And if so, why had he chosen not to?

Lynda repeated her question.

"Why didn't you say anything tonight? Don't you think people at least deserve to know your side of the story?"

"I don't know. I felt so overwhelmed. I was afraid of what might come out. I was angry and insulted, and I trusted her .. . and I just couldn't find the energy or the words. And in spite of it all, I didn't want to make her wrong to make me right."

Lynda felt her frustration ebb. Maybe he should've said something earlier, or even tonight, but he was allowed to make mistakes. Sometimes, big ones. Just because he was a leader didn't mean he had all the answers. Especially when his own emotions were triggered. He spoke again. "I've always wanted to be a 'good boy,' so I shut down to keep the peace." Lynda's reply was swift.

"Sometimes we have to take a stand for what's right. It's called 'Tough Love.' I know it can be difficult to tell someone you're disappointed or angry with them. It may not feel like you're coming from love, but sometimes speaking your truth in a loving way is the most loving thing you can do." As she spoke, she noticed Mel's eyes taking on a new clarity and determination, as if fog was clearing.

Somewhere along the way, Mel and Cindy came to see their roles and responsibilities differently. Cindy was a great role model and leader *in* the course room, while Mel endeavored to live the principles every day, *out* in the real world. When he had witnessed her behaving out of integrity with those principles, he had failed to hold her accountable. And others, too. Why had he avoided confrontation? Had he been overly concerned with keeping the peace? After Myrna died, that changed. His voice grew stronger. And some didn't seem to like it.

"I haven't had clear boundaries with Cindy, and I've let her walk right through them. And I can see now that it just enabled her to continue."

Lynda had never experienced problems like this in the community before, and she was mindful to stay positive and not get sucked into her old pattern of negative self-talk, or as she'd learned to call it, the "itty bitty shitty committee." But in the midst of her betrayal and hurt, a new sense of acceptance began to emerge. She'd planted its seeds long before the rift within the Community began.

But now it began to blossom into a form of personal truth that can only be earned through hardship. In many ways, she had Cindy and her allies to thank. It was their behavior that finally made the line between what was her responsibility and what wasn't crystal clear. And it showed her how strong she could really be.

She also knew that they had forced Mel to find his voice, his courage even. He became aware that avoiding confrontation had only enabled inappropriate behavior, and he hadn't created the closeness he thought he was preserving. She was proud of him. And of herself.

Soon enough, they'd need to draw on their new strength even more.

CHAPTER FIFTY-SIX
LETTERS

Lynda's heart skipped a beat. "Did she just write what I think she did?"

Mel grimaced, shaking his head in disbelief. They were standing at Lynda's computer and trying to digest a disgruntled email from an RYL grad. It was addressed to both Mel and Cindy. Even though the writer hadn't attended the infamous Steering Committee meeting, she uncannily expressed the very same complaints Debbie had outlined, until she wrote, *And, on the personality side, there is the long history of male behavior preferring young females on their arm, while discarding the older woman.*

"While discarding the older woman?" Mel read out loud in a quiet voice, almost to himself.

"Is she implying that you rejected any possible romance with a woman your own age? Who does she think you snubbed? Herself? Cindy?"

"I don't know," Mel answered, sounding disoriented. "I'm not sure she meant to, but that's what it sounds like."

Lynda couldn't believe the insensitivity it would take to suggest such a thing. Lynda knew Patty well, and never would've believed her capable of writing such an indignity, if it weren't right in front of her. She was familiar with her friend's direct, no-frills manner. Patty, like Lynda, shared a genuine commitment to integrate RYL principles into life. But this email was the opposite of that. It was painful to look at.

RYL taught people to put aside their self-serving stories and move beyond being a victim. One way this is accomplished is through open and honest communication with the intent to understand, to empathize. It was *a different way of being in the world* that required a deeply-felt process of freeing oneself of unconscious hidden agendas, aggressions, and assumptions. And it was a *practice* – a skill they tested and learned together in community.

"And, what do your finances have to do with increasing enrollment?" Lynda was referring to another troubling suggestion: *Perhaps someone's own personal finance issues are what's driving this seeming push to enroll.*

"*Seeming* push to enroll? What am I supposed to do with this?" As he looked at her in dismay, Lynda felt her face flush with protectiveness, anger, and exasperation. When would the aggression end?

"I feel so upset and angry right now," she said. Then she leveled her gaze. "How are you going to respond? What would you say?"

"Well, I don't want to respond in an email. I want to treat this respectfully, so I think I should get together with her personally." Lynda nodded in agreement. "But we have to finish getting ready for California, so there's no time right now. It will have to wait until we get back."

Lynda knew they weren't going to ask her *why* she wrote the email, or about the terrible insinuations. The goal of the conversation would be to honor her feelings while holding a space of loving compassion in order to find common ground. But, the similarity of this email to Debbie's speech made Lynda wonder if this narrative of *Mel making decisions without consulting Cindy* was spreading.

Mel and Lynda understood that it was human nature to create a narrative or "story" that fits one's personal belief system. We seek out evidence that validates our beliefs, and ignore evidence that doesn't support them, even though the belief may not be accurate.

After she and Mel read the email, they talked about the nature of their own evolving narrative and concluded that some of these accusations were tinged with jealousy and judgment on the part of people they once believed, perhaps mistakenly, to be their friends.

The evidence for this had mounted until they simply couldn't ignore it any longer. The situation was not going to resolve itself. And this latest email, which fully exposed the irrationality of what they were up against, was just more evidence.

Mel and Lynda had time to decide how they wanted to respond appropriately to Patty's email, and by the time they were in California, they were ready. Thursday evening, the day before the course began, they sat on the balcony overlooking Mission Viejo. While enjoying a glass of wine, they drafted a reply, which they hoped reflected RYL core values.

> *I shared your email with Lynda & it stirred emotions in us. We would prefer to get together and talk in person so that you can help us understand what you are feeling & what you want to accomplish in your email.*

What they got in return was a final denial. Patty wrote that she'd already spoken with Cindy and had no interest in seeing Mel or Lynda. "I believe my email has served its purpose." When Lynda read this, she sighed. All the anger, hurt, and confusion of the past couple of weeks bubbled up again. She remembered how elated she was to share her happiness with her friends when her relationship with Mel began. She never imagined the disapproval and rejection it would bring to the surface.

She was seeing people for who they really were now.

Her relationship with Mel was nothing like the gossip portrayed it. Lynda wondered, were these women validating one another, swapping stories and winding each other up? She pondered her life. Her mother, her children, relationships, career, and her dreams. All of her choices had been steppingstones that brought her here to this balcony, to her life with Mel. Now, she understood that the conflict surrounding her issued an invitation, *an opportunity from which to learn*. Even though she was a little shocked and unsettled by the course of events, it was contrastingly joyful to find the strength to follow her heart. To live with eyes and heart wide open.

Follow your heart. It was easy advice to give, but often challenging to follow through. It took nerve to be willing to be disliked and judged, and to learn to hold your own hand through it all. Some people wanted to make her wrong for loving Mel. Instead, they were teaching her to know who she was and to stand in her truth.

She'd spent her life trying to figure out how to do just that. Though learning this lesson came at a price, it was one she was willing to pay, one she was now strong enough to face. As she watched a pale star blink like a cosmic firefly through the California night sky, she smiled and topped off their glasses.

Something, or someone, had brought them together. And this greater mystery, whatever it was, would help them. They were following their hearts and they had faith they would be supported on their path.

CHAPTER FIFTY-SEVEN
SHARK IN THE WATER

While the following day was controversial for some, for Lynda it was the start of a new chapter. It was her first day being a substitute RYL instructor. And it thrilled Mel to spend it supporting her and the students. After the flurry of emails, it was also a relief, and he found himself enjoying the familiarity of the RYL course room, no matter what city he was in.

He knew he needed to deescalate the situation with Cindy when he returned to Tampa. He'd come to terms with the fact that the issues weren't just going to blow over, as he once hoped. He'd shepherded the community through conflict and bumps in the past but nothing like this. The recent emails revealed that there was real damage occurring, and he was just starting to grasp its full effects. Still, he found a question from one of the emails particularly insightful. Perhaps this was because it was a good one and contained a potentially hard truth.

Many of those who knew and loved Myrna are still actively grieving, and the loss of her presence is keenly felt. With this loss in mind, how can you best provide leadership to continue RYL from here?

The truth was that the impasse was complicated. But this question addressed an aspect of it he needed to think about. He hadn't anticipated how profoundly someone's grief over Myrna could influence their perceptions of his choices as he began his own new chapter. He suspected that some of the turmoil started here, and he could understand that. He'd been engrossed in his own grief as well as recovering from the sheer exhaustion of caretaking. Now, with Lynda's help, he began to see their perspective.

What the community knew was that one of their beloved leaders, maybe a parental figure for some, died, and five months later her widowed husband began a relationship with one of their own. And Lynda *was* a younger woman compared to many of the others. He could see how it could trigger some people's past with their own family dramas. However, he also knew that he wasn't responsible for other people's feelings.

All the same, it had affected the community on his watch, and for that he could assume some accountability. While he realized it wasn't his responsibility to anticipate the potential issues some might experience around Myrna's death, he still wondered how he might have helped avoid them.

He knew he and Lynda still had many friends and supporters. And he believed that most of those who were not supporters did not intend to be malicious. He suspected grief had made them vulnerable, that the situation with Lynda had confused and triggered them, and with no one to guide them, they fell into the trap of gossip and blame.

If a grad had come directly to Mel with an issue with another person, he would have guided them through the RYL process of examining their own feelings to get to the root of the problem. But when it was Mel himself whom others had an issue with, he perceived it differently. He concluded that in defending himself, he would be making the other person wrong. He saw it as a choice of "being right or being close," and he made the choice to be close. Looking back, he saw how he'd "turned the other cheek" instead of confronting another with their own misconceptions. He realized that this behavior hadn't set a good example for the community, and it had contributed in leading them all to this point. Things had irrevocably changed, and he'd played a part.

Now, knowing this, all he could do was move forward.

How *would* he provide the best leadership from here?

A few days after he returned to Tampa, he received a call from his friend Becky. He perked up when he heard her easy, refreshing voice. She was one of those people who had a gift for not taking herself too seriously. Even when the other grads called her "Bossy Becky," she'd just smile and get in on the fun. After everything that had happened, he realized how much he appreciated her. She felt safe. He could trust her. After exchanging a few pleasantries, her voice grew quiet, tentative.

"Listen Mel, I'm calling to ask you. Well, say someone heard rumors . . . things they suspected weren't true. What should they do? Should they interfere or is it other people's stuff?" She was referring to a basic RYL principle in which each of us is responsible for our own life and our own happiness, and not responsible for others' happiness.

"Depends. If the rumors are harmful, then maybe that person should interfere. Because there could be more at risk of harm than just one relationship." Becky took a few moments to consider this before asking her next question.

"But what about other people's stuff? If someone talks about rumors they're hearing but it doesn't directly involve them, aren't they getting into other people's stuff?" At this, Mel began to feel wary, not of Becky, but of the distinct possibility that her question wasn't hypothetical.

"That's a good question. What about this? Say I'm in the ocean, and I'm swimming, and my friend is there, and they see some minnows behind me. What do they do?"

"Nothing, I guess. The minnows can't hurt you."

"Right. But say I'm in the water and there's a shark behind me. What do they do then?" He paused and waited, but she didn't reply. "I would hope that my friend would yell, Shark!"

"Okay," she said. "Shark."

Mel asked her to tell him more, and that's when the story came out. Mel expected it to be about his supposedly inappropriate relationship with Lynda. What he heard instead shook him to the core. "There are people saying that you're taking money from the company to pay for your RV. It's going around in some emails." He heard uneasiness in her words as he grit his teeth.

"Who?"

"Patty for one. She invited me to her house and told me I needed to see something. When I got there, she showed me some emails circulating between her and a few others. One of them actually had the amount of money you pay for your RV each month." This new information revealed that the idle gossip had become a smear. And Patty was more involved than he thought.

To establish the legitimacy of the email chain, he asked Becky what the RV payment was, and she confirmed it. Mel knew that no one had access to this financial information except for Cindy. His heart sank. The source could only be Cindy. "Look," he heard Becky say, her voice sounding far away. "I don't want to be involved in this."

"I know, but you're calling me. You're already involved." He thought fast. The flames of deceit and mistrust were blowing out of control, and it was imperative that he not do anything that might fan them. The situation, while unbearable, presented a real opportunity to halt the poison of gossip and nebulous, second-hand information. Mel reasoned that Becky needed to approach Cindy so Cindy would get the email chain story first-hand. He wanted to gauge how Cindy reacted when confronted with the possibility of the leak.

"I have a request. This isn't good for any of us, as you know. I'm going to talk to Cindy about it, but how would you feel about taking this information to her before I do? *You* saw the email. *You* have the concern about negative gossip. So, it's only right that you take it to her directly, so as a leader, she has a chance to address it."

Becky was hesitant. But she also knew in her heart that the gossip was against RYL principles, besides being untrue. She saw what it was doing to the community, and she felt the need for someone to stop it. Becky wanted to help, but said she'd need a little more time to think about it.

When he opened his email the next morning, he found a much needed note of comfort and support.

Melvyn, having slept on it, my answer is still yes. Thank you for bleeding for me. I will stand up and be counted. Beck.

CHAPTER FIFTY-EIGHT
MORE THAN READY

By the time Mel was pulling up to meet Cindy at their favorite Thai restaurant a few days later, he had all the information he needed. Becky had met with Cindy and told her about the slander. And Cindy had denied knowing anything about it.

He was certain she was the only person who could've shared the exact amount of the RV payment, for he included it in their monthly cash flow report. When he prepared the report, he made sure to divide the net profit into their agreed upon cuts. While the Loft payment was included, it was a separate line item that came out of his cut. It was never expensed from the business.

Regardless, the rumors of financial mismanagement and stealing had already caused harm, and he was unsure how to address it. He'd talked with Lynda about whether he should attempt damage control in the wider community or not. And he'd considered sending a mass email in an attempt to set the record straight, as Lynda had suggested, but he felt it might create its own problems. The community had hundreds of members, and there was no way to determine how many had been affected by the unrest and gossip. He was sure it wasn't everyone, especially the newest members. Even at the Steering Committee meeting, not everyone had understood, or had known the backstory about what occurred.

The turmoil was thickest among those closest to Cindy, a group of friends that had grown in number, but certainly didn't represent the majority of the community. He was morbidly aware that there was no right way to handle the situation, though there seemed to be plenty of wrong ways. And many of those who were involved had already made up their minds, and anything he did or said, especially via an email, would most likely be used to feed their drama, not bring understanding.

He thought about all the people who might feel as if they were in the crossfire, having to decide what was right and where they stood. Just like he was. They had a lot to lose, too. Friends, allies, community. Perhaps more than anything, the refuge RYL had been for many of them – and still could be. It wasn't an easy thing.

It was most important to act in the best interest of the community in the way he handled this state of affairs with Cindy, and all the players who were involved. When all was said and done, he wanted every action he took to reflect this, even if no one recognized or acknowledged it. It was crucial that he practice his own teachings rigorously at such a difficult time, because this was exactly when they were most needed.

He still invited the opportunity to speak personally with anyone who asked him about the rumors, and he still held hope that those who maligned him would choose being close over being right. Still, he wasn't going to turn the other cheek or allow the untruths to fester anymore.

And it started with confronting Cindy.

As he spotted her car glinting in a parking space nearby, he knew this meeting was the last chance at salvaging their relationship.

His hope was that Cindy would own up to her misconduct. In the best of worlds, it could even be used as a teaching tool. If they reconciled and righted things enough, they could take this lesson into the course room and use it to demonstrate their own imperfections as a path to growth.

Over the years, he'd done it plenty of times. He used his bankruptcy, his infidelity, the Iceman – all of it – as tools for growth in the course room. Revealing his greatest vulnerabilities, his weaknesses and failures – this was part of his humanity. How could he expect to help anyone to move from judgement into love if they were never confronted with the shadowy parts of themselves they so wanted to repress and to judge?

While he hoped she would be, if she wasn't willing to take responsibility for her actions, he realized their business partnership was probably over. How could he trust her? And how could he stand beside her in the course room, teaching the RYL values and practices he held so dear in his heart, knowing what she'd done to him and to the community? Knowing how far she could go?

How could that be in integrity?

The crazy thing was that he didn't feel sad about it anymore. He was exhausted, and he just wanted resolution so he could move forward. Whatever happened between them was far less important than ensuring RYL's survival.

As he walked towards her, Patty's question still echoed through his mind. *How can you best provide leadership to continue RYL from here?* He was finally on the verge of knowing, unequivocally, the answer.

Shadows smudged Cindy's normally spacious grin as he sat down opposite her. The mood was predictably somber, and aside from ordering drinks they dispensed with pleasantries and got right into the emails Becky had reported. Cindy, who probably thought that was all they were there to discuss, sipped her coffee and spoke first.

"I was deeply shocked when Becky came to me," she said in dulcet tones. "I honestly cannot imagine how Patty got that information. And the gossip?" She raised her eyebrows, shaking her head in disgust. Mel realized she was going to preserve the pretense that their dinner meeting was about gossip among the grads instead of the breakdown in their relationship and her role in it. He steadied his voice.

"Cindy, I've never told any of the grads what the payment is. The only place that information is located is the monthly cash flow reports. And the only people who have access to those reports are you and me. What I'm wondering is how would anyone know that information." He stared at her, waiting for an answer. He so wanted her to just be honest. Cindy's forehead pinched inward. She seemed nervous as she tried to keep the focus on the rumors, not their cause.

"I don't know. All of this is just so . . . distasteful." She rubbed her brow as if she was trying to massage a headache.

"That I agree with." Mel's words were heavy with meaning. Whatever place this came from within her, he remained utterly mystified. They'd created their business with the best of intentions, and Mel was grateful for their ten years together. Yet as he regarded her, he was distracted by the surreal impression that he was gazing at a complete stranger. When does someone known to you become unknown to you, he wondered. How is it even possible?

"Who shared the emails with Becky again?" Cindy asked, pecking at her salad. When she heard Patty's name, she waved her hand dismissively. "Oh, she doesn't have many friends, anyway."

Whatever role Patty had played, Cindy's response provoked protectiveness from Mel. Patty was a human being worthy of equal respect. As community leaders, he and Cindy were in a position to guide and serve her, not belittle her. Not define her worth on any kind of status.

What disturbed him the most was that after ten years of working together, he was left to imagine her real motivation, because he realized now that she would never tell him. Any admission would require her to take responsibility for her actions.

RYL's mission was to move the consciousness of mankind from judgment to love. People needed learning opportunities, safe places, to make that choice, over and over again. To grow strong.

Would they judge or would they choose love?

Would they hide or would they tell the truth?

Who would they be when all was said and done?

Mel sighed. Cindy seemed to have made her choice. At least for today.

He felt himself hyper-focusing on the tables around him, on the people stabbing noodles and shaking spicy oil on their food. He had nothing left to say. Her opportunity to take responsibility, to be honest, had run its course. He knew he felt taken advantage of and under-appreciated only because he'd permitted the situation. He'd allowed it. Now, it was untenable.

He could no longer, in conscience, stand beside her and teach anything, especially RYL. Not ever again.

As the conversation unraveled to bits, oxygen seemed to flood his brain, every step in front of him materializing more clearly. Even before he stepped away from the table, and from his ten-year partnership with Cindy, he began unravelling the details of buying her out and moving forward.

He knew the process would be long, and at times frustrating, but he felt certain the worst was already in his rear-view mirror. He was now free to continue his mission, to serve others, and to rebuild his community. And though he didn't fully comprehend the challenges of rebuilding, he knew he'd take it day by day, month by month, course by course. Just like he always had. The anger and hurt of the past few months began to melt into deep release, and even awe for the journey he'd taken over the past year. Now, after everything, there would be no need to clear his good name.

There would be *only* his good name.

The refrain he'd voiced so many times to countless students replaced Patty's question of how he could best provide leadership.

Are you ready? Only this time, he was the one answering, not asking. And he was.

He was more than ready.

CHAPTER FIFTY-NINE
FRUIT ON THE TREES

A few months later on a sunny June morning, Lynda opened her RYL for Couples instructor notebook and regarded her students. Most sat at tables, while a few huddled or reclined together on plump floor cushions. She'd been a part of count-less courses over the past nine years, as student, assistant, and instructor. Now, she was teaching her first Couple's Course. She'd seen many people move in and out of the community in that time. So many who learned to love themselves slowly, with humility and great fierceness.

None more so than she. She cleared her throat and spoke to the class about the importance of a shared vision.

"We're going to do one of my favorite exercises. You're going to make a list with your partner, and on it, I want you to write your shared goals and dreams for your future." Lynda smiled over at Mel, who was standing a few feet away from her.

"And all the things you want to manifest together," Mel added, placing special emphasis on *together*.

She knew exactly how it felt to be handed a pencil and told to list all your dreams – the exhilaration of possibility and hope, mixed with a little fear. As was her habit, she used humor to ease any potential anxiety.

"No pressure!" She laughed with the students. She knew well how much pressure it could be to state your dreams and to stand up for them. To yourself, to others. "We'll go for as long as you need, and Mel or I will be around to check on you. If you have a question, just call on us, and we'll come to you. Before you get started, I'd like to share a quote with you: *If you want to get the fruit on the tree, you have to be willing to go out on a limb.*" She paused a moment to allow everyone time to take it in. "And the reason I'm sharing it with you today is because I want each of you, as individuals, to be fearless as you make your list with your partner. Be true to yourself as you take your partner's hand and walk out on that limb together."

They seemed encouraged as they began speaking quietly and scribbling. Lynda drew to the side of the classroom and took out a pencil. "I think we should make our list, too," she suggested to Mel, who had followed her. He beamed.

"Well, we are a couple. And we of all people know that lists work," he said with his characteristic dry humor that managed to be both awkward and charming. Lynda felt warm as she recalled the first time she placed her own Ideal Partner list beside his and compared them.

She would always remember that night as proof that something right and true, invisible and impossibly faithful, had held her all her life. Until she could grow into her own strength, her own destiny, her own passion. Mel sat down beside her.

"Where should we start?" he asked gently. Lynda considered the question carefully. Most great endeavors seemed to start with that very inquiry.

She thought about how Mel had nearly completed the process of severing his business partnership, effectively making him the sole owner of the company. It had been a relatively smooth process with the occasional bump in the road, but it didn't disconcert either of them now and hadn't for some time.

Mel and Lynda had worked together to bring closure to the split with Cindy. They chose to focus on the gratitude they felt for the years of friendship and all the lives that had been touched in a profound way. By allowing things to end positively without bitterness and blame, they created the space to discover the beauty of the next chapter. Perhaps this is why she and Mel had recently started talking more seriously about moving somewhere together. About a new vision in a new place. Lynda hovered her pencil over the paper.

"We've both always wanted to live in the mountains. Why not start there?" Mel nodded in agreement as a rogue ray of sunlight burst through the window and splashed the paper. "And let's write a book. About all of it. About you, me, and Myrna. About everything that happened. About how love can look when you surrender, trust the process, and follow your heart."

"I can't imagine anything better," he whispered as she began writing.

THE REST OF OUR STORY

July 4, 2008, Lynda and Mel were married in a garden ceremony at their home in Tampa. Florida. Surrounded by family and friends, it was a beautiful and joyous celebration with dancing and laughter. And the city put on a firework show to cap off the evening! They honeymooned on a week-long western Caribbean cruise, enjoying fun adventures of swimming with turtles in Grand Cayman, exploring the island of Cozumel, and cave tubing in Belize.

One of the goals they had set for themselves in the *Our Ideal Relationship* exercise in that first *Couples Course* was to move to the mountains. Lynda and Mel traveled out west to scout out the Rocky Mountains in Colorado as well as visited the Blue Ridge Mountains of North Carolina, and in the fall of 2009, followed their hearts and moved into their new home in Maggie Valley, NC.

Settling into the community, Lynda found work teaching exercise classes at the Waynesville Recreation Center as well as serving BBQ at Butts on the Creek, a popular local eatery—just until she built up her new massage practice. Mel started networking with other local business owners, and in February 2010 he taught his first Asheville RYL seminar and began building the Asheville RYL community. New friendships blossomed, unfamiliar paths were explored, favorite stomping grounds discovered, and before long Maggie Valley was truly *home*.

And the journey continues.......

ABOUT THE AUTHORS

Mel Fergenbaum and Lynda Saffell are teachers who are dedicated to helping others realize their full potential as well as visionaries who are passionate about creating global oneness and a new way of living in the world. Through creating acceptance of ourselves, open honesty in our families, and responsibility in our communities, we create harmony in our world and begin to shift the consciousness of man from judgement to love.

Life Transforming Opportunities with Mel Fergenbaum
Mel received his training with Global Relationships Center and was certified as a Group Facilitator in 1995. Founded in 2000, MC Insights' signature course was the REDIRECT YOUR LIFE Experience, a weekend seminar of profound and shared

learning experiences. Mel's work has evolved to a one-on-one mentoring program, helping people with both personal and professional concerns. Sessions and workshops are available both online and in person.

Mentoring with Mel
Communication for Couples workshops and weekend retreats
Finding Your Personal Power workshops
Contact: mobile 727-580-1842, email mel@mcinsightsinc.com
Website: www.MCInsightsInc.com

Self-Care and Transformational Opportunities with Lynda Saffell
Lynda is a holistic health practitioner who believes in treating the whole person – body, mind, emotions, and spirit – for ultimate health and wellbeing. Along with her fine-tuned skill of "listening" to your body, she incorporates strength & balance training, massage therapy, yoga and meditation, healthy eating, and yoga therapy. Sessions and workshops are available both online and in person.

Phoenix Rising Yoga Therapy private sessions
Meditation classes, private sessions and workshops
Group Exercise Classes Yoga, Pilates, Strength & Balance, Flexibility training, Dance Party
Communication for Couples workshops and weekend retreats
Contact: mobile 813-629-1835, email Lynda.Saffell@gmail.com
Website: LyndaSaffell.MassageTherapy.com

Mel and Lynda are also available for speaking engagements and book signings.

Life is a journey and love makes that journey worthwhile.
Author Unknown

Honeymoon Cruise, Cozumel, Mexico, July 2008